Green Transportation and Energy Consumption in China

T0331289

This book provides insights into China's energy consumption and pollution as well as its energy saving policies. It explores energy saving ways and argues for an energy consumption revolution, which includes technologies to improve transportation resource efficiency, modification of existing transportation infrastructure and structure.

This book uses various analytical models to study the relationships within the transportation system. It also includes comparative analysis of China, Japan, the US and developing countries on traffic demand and transportation energy consumption. This book highlights the urgent need to review China's current transportation policies in order to secure a breakthrough in energy saving and emissions reduction.

Jian Chai is Professor at the School of Economics and Management, Xidian University, Xi'an, China.

Ying Yang is a PhD candidate at the School of Management, Xi'an Jiaotong University, Xi'an, China.

Quanying Lu is currently pursuing a master's degree at the International Business School of Shaanxi Normal University, Xi'an, China.

Limin Xing is currently pursuing a master's degree at the International Business School of Shaanxi Normal University, Xi'an, China.

Ting Liang is currently pursuing a master's degree at the International Business School of Shaanxi Normal University, Xi'an, China.

Kin Keung Lai is currently Professor at the International Business School of Shaanxi Normal University, Xi'an, China.

Shouyang Wang is currently a Professor and Dean at the College of Economics and Management, University of Chinese Academy of Sciences, Beijing, China. He is also the Director of Forecasting Science Research Center at the Chinese Academy of Sciences, Beijing, China.

Routledge Advances in Risk Management
Edited by Kin Keung Lai and Shouyang Wang

Green Transportation and Energy Consumption in China

Jian Chai, Ying Yang, Quanying Lu, Limin Xing, Ting Liang, Kin Keung Lai and Shouyang Wang

Routledge
Taylor & Francis Group

LONDON AND NEW YORK

First published 2017 by Routledge

2 Park Square, Milton Park, Abingdon, Oxfordshire OX14 4RN

52 Vanderbilt Avenue, New York, NY 10017

Routledge is an imprint of the Taylor & Francis Group, an informa business

First issued in paperback 2019

British Library Cataloguing-in-Publication Data
A catalogue record for this book is available from the British Library

Library of Congress Cataloging-in-Publication Data
A catalog record for this book has been requested

ISBN: 978-1-138-03733-5 (hbk)
ISBN: 978-0-367-37478-5 (pbk)

Typeset in Galliard
by Apex CoVantage, LLC

Contents

Figures

Tables

1 China's transportation energy consumption

An overview

Transportation energy conservation and emissions reduction are global concerns. Whether in developed or developing countries, motor traffic is the main source of outdoor air pollution in cities. Every year, over 2 million people worldwide die from excessively inhaling small particles from the air. Among all the continents, the air pollution in Asia is the worst. Among the 15 cities with the worst particulate pollution in the world, 12 are located in Asia, and transportation has become one of the main sources of air pollution in these cities, with traffic pollution being the source of much fossil fuel consumption. According to a research report from the Center for International Climate and Environmental Research – Oslo (CICERO), issued with the National Academy of Sciences (www.cicero.uio.no/en/about), currently, exhaust emissions from motor vehicles, ships, airplanes and trains are main factors in global warming. Over the past ten years, CO_2 emissions have increased by 13 per cent worldwide; however, the increase rate of carbon emissions from transportation reaches 25 per cent. While other industrial sectors are formulating emissions reduction objectives, traffic pollution remains hard to curb because the transportation sector is controlled by hundreds of millions of people. For example, the EU successfully reduced emissions in most industrial sectors, except for transportation, and carbon emissions from the transportation sector in the EU has increased by 21 per cent over the past ten years. Obviously, transportation energy conservation and emissions reduction have become significant challenges for most countries in the world. As for China, a major developing country, with the acceleration of industrialization and urbanization, issues of transportation energy conservation and emissions reduction have become more and more important.

1.1 The current situation and structure change in China's transportation

1.1.1 Passenger transportation development

From 1990 to 2012, Chinese passenger turnover maintained sustained and rapid growth. As shown in Figure 1.1, passenger turnover increased to 3.39 trillion passengers/km in 2012 from 562.84 billion passengers/km in 1990, while the

billion passengers/km

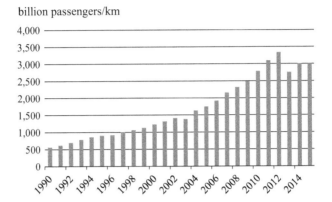

Figure 1.1 Chinese passenger traffic turnover from 1990 to 2015

Source: China National Bureau of Statistics, *China Statistical Yearbook* (2016).

Note: Road passenger turnover includes the number of operating passenger cars but does not include (electric) busses or taxis on city roads. Similarly, rail does not include urban rail transit (subways), and civil aviation does not include international routes. However, domestic civil aviation routes include routes between China and Hong Kong after 1997 as well as routes with Macao after 1999.

average annual growth was 8.5 per cent. Although passenger turnover fell sharply to 2.76 trillion passengers/km in 2013, the level of reduction was 17.41 per cent compared with 2012. The experience of developed countries has shown that both productive passenger demand and consumer demand have been showing rapid growth during urbanization, and productive passenger demand growth will slow in the middle and later periods. Today, China is in a stage of rapid urbanization, as whole society mobility increases passenger turnover growth.

On the one hand, with the rapid expansion of urban populations and with improvement in living standards, the growth potential of passenger transportation demand is huge. On the other hand, unbalanced regional development has led to the increasing flow of regional personnel. By 2020, passenger turnover will continue rapid growth momentum (Zhang, Xiong and Kang, 2015). In recent years, the prosperity of the tourism market also led to increased traffic passenger turnover. In 2015, the number of Chinese domestic tourist trips increased to 4 billion from 784 million in 2001, enjoying a compound growth rate of 12.34 per cent. Tourism revenue grew from 3.52 billion RMB in 2001 to 34.2 billion RMB of 2015, enjoying a compound growth rate of 17.63 per cent. But from the perspective of the residential travel rate, the average travel frequency per person every year, which was 2.98 in 2015, there are still large gaps compared to developed countries, which has a per capita travel rate 8 times greater.

In recent years, the passenger market structure has also undergone great change. Before 2012, road passenger turnover occupied a dominant position in all types of transportation modes, 55.32 per cent of road passenger turnover in all types of transportation in 2012 (Figure 1.2), and rail passenger turnover accounts

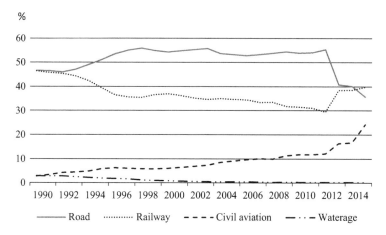

Figure 1.2 Structural change in passenger transport turnover in China
Source: China National Bureau of Statistics, *China Statistical Yearbook* (2016).

for 29.4 per cent. During the period from 2013 to 2015, the proportion of road passenger turnover decreased significantly, accounting for 40.81 per cent, 40.15 per cent and 35.74 per cent respectively. During this period, highway passenger turnover increased from 981.23 billion passengers/km in 2012 to 1,059.56 billion passengers/km, a proportional increase of 39.8 per cent, surpassing road passenger turnover. This is mainly due to rapid development of high-speed rail in China in recent years: by the end of 2015, the operating mileage of China's high-speed rail system achieved more than 18,000 km of track. China's high-speed railway network is the world's largest and enjoys highest operating speed, utilizing a basic shape with "four vertical" trunks. High-speed rail passenger turnover increased from 1.56 billion passengers/km in 2008 to 386.34 billion passengers/km in 2015, and the ratio of high-speed rail to railway passenger turnover increased from 0.2 per cent in 2008 to 32.3 per cent in 2015.

1.1.2 Freight transportation development

From 1990 to 2012, the turnover of freight traffic in China continued to grow rapidly (Figure 1.3), increasing from 262.8 billion tons/km in 1990 to 1,737.77 billion tons/km in 2012, with an average annual growth rate of 7.93 per cent. The sudden decline in freight turnover occurred in 2013, which was mainly due to the reduction in road freight turnover in 2013. The turnover of road freight in 2013 decreased from 5,953.49 billion tons/km in 2012 to 5,573.88 billion tons/km, with a descending rate of 6.38 per cent. In the previous period (1990–2012), road freight turnover maintained high growth, with an average annual growth rate of 17.31 per cent. Second, in 2012, the volume of water cargo turnover and railway cargo turnover declined slightly by 2.78 per

Million tons/km

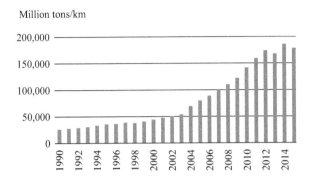

Figure 1.3 China's freight turnover from 1990 to 2015

Source: China National Bureau of Statistics, *China Statistical Yearbook* (2016).

%

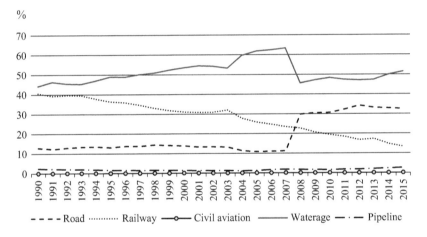

- - - - Road   ·········· Railway   —o— Civil aviation   ——— Waterage   — · — Pipeline

Figure 1.4 Structural change of freight turnover in China

Source: China National Bureau of Statistics, *China Statistical Yearbook* (2016).

cent and 0.05 per cent respectively. The turnover of civil aviation cargo and postal cargo increased by 3.91 per cent and 10.3 per cent, respectively, over the same period.

According to the same measures, structural changes in freight turnover in China from 1990 to 2007 are mainly reflected in the increase of water transport and the decline of railways (Figure 1.4), while the proportion of highway, civil aviation and pipeline transportation has not changed much. According to revised highway statistics in 2008, in the volume of freight traffic of 2015, highway, railway, civil aviation, water transport and pipeline traffic accounted for 32.5 per cent, 13.32 per cent, 0.12 per cent, 51.45 per cent and 2.62 per cent respectively (China National Bureau of Statistics, *China Statistical Yearbook*, 2016).

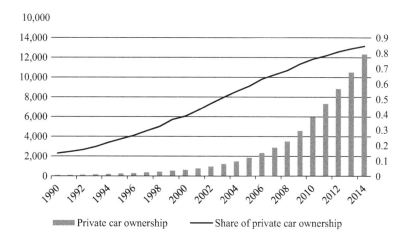

Figure 1.5 Ownership and share of private cars in China

Source: China National Bureau of Statistics, *China Statistical Yearbook* (2015).

1.1.3 Urban traffic development

As can be seen from Figure 1.5, the share of private car ownership in China's urban transport sector increased exponentially in 1990–2014, from 816,200 car owners to 123,393,600, an average annual growth rate of 14.7 per cent. The proportion of private car ownership to all civilian vehicles increased from 14.8 per cent in 1990 to 84.5 per cent in 2014. This data shows that China's automobile market structure has undergone fundamental changes, with individual residents becoming the main consumers in China's auto market. With the rapid development of China's economy, income levels continued to increase, especially the incomes of urban residents, and private car ownership has also increased, while mortgage loans and a series of driving measures, such as deep tax discounts for low-emissions vehicle purchases and scrapped car subsidies, have also promoted private car ownership. However, the rapid increase in the number of private cars has also exacerbated urban problems, such as traffic congestion and urban air pollution. In recent years, serious fog and hazy weather have been closely related to motor vehicle exhaust emissions. The linear growth of car ownership has made congestion in Beijing and other cities more and more serious, and as automobile concentration increases, so do exhaust emissions.

1.2 Transportation energy consumption and carbon emissions

1.2.1 Energy consumption in China's transportation sector

According to IEA statistics, from 1990–2013, China's transportation terminal energy consumption was accelerating trend. In the 1990s, China's transportation

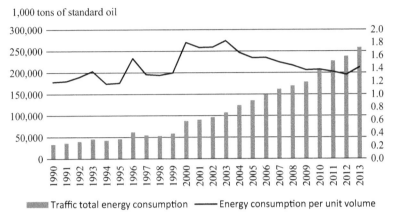

1,000 tons of standard oil

Figure 1.6 Energy consumption and transportation energy intensity (1,000 tons of standard oil per 100 metric tons/km) for terminal transportation in China from 1990–2013

Source: International Energy Agency (IEA), 2015.

terminal energy consumption increased from 33,454 tons of standard oil in 1990 to 87.9 billion tons of standard oil in 2000, with an annual growth rate of about 7 per cent (Figure 1.6). In the twenty-first century, China's transportation terminal energy consumption growth has accelerated significantly, an average annual growth rate was 8.7 per cent from 2000 to 2013. China's transportation terminal energy consumption reached 258,301 tons of standard oil in 2013, almost double the consumption in 2000, and 80 per cent of China's current energy consumption is concentrated in road traffic.

Corresponding to the total transportation terminal energy consumption, from 1990 to 2000, the energy intensity of transportation in China increased from 1.19 tons of standard oil per 100 million tons in 1990 to 1.8 tons of standard oil per 100 million tons in 2003. Since then, it declined slightly and then rose to 1.83 in 2003, and then it has been in a downward transition. The energy intensity of traffic was 1.3 kiloton of standard oil per 100 million tons/km in 2012, 1.42 kiloton of standard oil per 100 million tons/km in 2013. It shows that, with the substitution of vehicles and the improvement of fuel quality, the energy intensity of traffic will decrease in the long run.

1.2.2 Carbon emissions in China's transportation sector

From overall trends shown in Figure 1.7, carbon dioxide (CO_2) emissions from transportation in China has increased rapidly from 1990 to 2013, from 120.62 million metric tons of CO_2 equivalent (MtCO$_2$ Eq.) in 1990 to 860.54 million tons of CO_2 equivalent in 2013, an average annual increase rate of 9.57 per cent, which is higher than the annual growth rate of total CO_2 emissions

Mt CO$_2$ Eq.

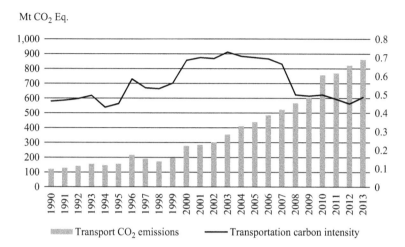

Figure 1.7 Total transport carbon emissions and transport CO$_2$ intensity (MtCO$_2$ Eq./100 million tons/km) in China from 1990 to 2013

Source: World Bank, Carbon Dioxide Information Analysis Center (n.d.)

Mt CO$_2$ Eq.

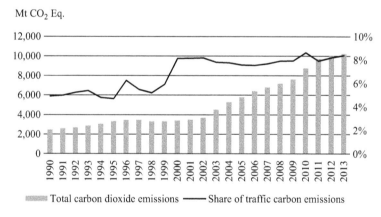

Figure 1.8 Total CO$_2$ emissions in China from 1990 to 2013

Source: World Bank, Carbon Dioxide Information Analysis Center (n.d.)

(6.55 per cent). China's total CO$_2$ emissions increased from 2,460.74 MtCO$_2$ Eq. in 1990 to 10,249.46 MtCO$_2$ Eq. in 2013, as shown in Figure 1.8. The proportion of transportation CO$_2$ emissions to total emissions increased from 4.64 per cent in 1990 to 8.4 per cent in 2013. Since 2000, CO$_2$ emissions from traffic have accelerated the growth rate: the annual average growth rate in 1990–1999 was 6.45 per cent, while from 2000 to 2013 the annual average growth rate was 11.58 per cent, an increase of 5.13 percentage points. Since 2000, the proportion of CO$_2$ emissions from traffic relative to total emissions began to fluctuate around 8 per cent. In terms of the intensity of carbon emissions, calculated by the ratio of metric tons of carbon dioxide equivalent ($MtCO_2$ Eq.) per kilometer, the overall trend shows first increase and then decrease. The intensity of transport carbon emissions increased from 0.464 in 1990 to 0.685 in 2000. Before the 2008 financial crisis, the intensity of carbon emissions from transportation was high, between 0.66 and 0.73 in 2001–2007; then, it decreased sharply from 0.66 in 2007 to 0.498 in 2008, decreasing more slowly after 2008.

1.3 Conclusion

1   Since the reform and opening up of China under Deng Xiaoping, with the rapid development of China's transportation industry, transportation infrastructure has been greatly improved, and passenger and cargo transport volume continue to grow rapidly. At present, China's passenger traffic is dominated by highways and railways. By 2015, roads and railways account for 39.8 per cent and 35.74 per cent respectively of passenger turnover. However, at a turning point in 2012, the proportion of roads started to decline, while the share of railway transportation has increased. And in recent years, civil aviation passenger traffic began to gradually increase in 2015, accounting for 24.23 per cent. At present, China's freight transport is mainly based on water transport and roads; passenger turnover in water transport and on highways accounted for 51.46 per cent and 32.49 per cent in 2015 respectively.

2   In recent years, China's transportation energy consumption has increased rapidly, holding an increasingly prominent position in China's energy consumption. China's transportation terminal energy consumption increased from 33,454 tons of standard oil in 1990 to 258,301 kilotons of standard oil in 2013, with an annual growth rate of about 9.9 per cent. According to the International Energy Agency (IEA), transportation has been the most energy-intensive sector in China for more than 20 years, more than double the national average growth rate (4.5 per cent); thus, the proportion of transportation energy consumption in the China's terminal energy consumption has increased significantly, from 5.6 per cent in 1990 to 14.5 per cent in 2013, and the position in the structure of China's energy consumption has become increasingly important (IEA, 2015). What's more, 80 per cent of China's current transportation energy consumption is concentrated in road traffic.

3   The rapid increase in transportation energy consumption has also led to a rapid increase in carbon dioxide (CO_2) emissions from the transportation sector. CO_2 emissions from the transportation sector rose from 120.62 million $MtCO_2$ Eq. in 1990 to 860.54 million tons, with an average annual growth rate of 9.57 per cent, higher than China's total annual CO_2 emissions growth rate of 6.55 per cent. The proportion of CO_2 emissions from the transportation sector to total emissions increased from 4.64 per cent in 1990 to 8.4 per cent in 2013. Regarding mode of transportation, CO_2 emissions

are mainly concentrated in road traffic, which accounted for 80 per cent of CO_2 emissions in 2011.

4   Transportation is the "harbinger" of economic development in the "new normal" economy, and maintaining the current high-speed development of China's economy is inseparable from the development of transportation. However, if current energy consumption and carbon dioxide emissions continue to increase, it will be difficult to achieve "green transport" objectives and meet climate change agreements. Energy saving emissions reduction in transportation is the key to promoting structural energy saving, through optimizing transportation structures to achieve energy saving emissions reduction. Therefore, studying the transportation industry, especially energy saving in road traffic, will have important practical significance.

2 The real drivers of road traffic demand in China

Air pollution from transportation, caused by its consumption of petroleum products, has become an important source of urban and regional haze, and traffic demand is a driving force behind transportation energy consumption, which causes air pollution. This chapter holds that studying influential factors in traffic demand is of great significance to alleviating the current air pollution caused by transportation. Based on this, this chapter establishes a structural equation model, using the Bayesian estimation method on two countries considered (China and the US), taking into account traffic infrastructure, transportation costs and economic activities as potential variables influencing road traffic demand. This chapter finds that the asymmetric effects of passenger demand and cargo demand are more apparent and that American consumers' expectations for prices differ greatly from expectations in China.

2.1 Introduction

At present, more than 50 per cent of the total consumption of oil in China is formed by transportation, and with lower energy consumption in industrial development and slower population growth, transportation will continue to drive the main momentum behind oil consumption growth. According to the China Association of Automobile Manufacturers (www.caam.org.cn/data/), starting in 2009, China was the world's superpower in motor vehicle production and sales for four years in a row. The *Annals of China's Motor Vehicle Pollution Prevention of 2013* shows that motor vehicle pollution has become an important source of air pollution and is the important cause of the haze, photochemical smog pollution, in China (Ministry of Environmental Protection, n.d.). With the rapid growth of car ownership, our environment will face challenges from transportation, especially highway transportation pollution caused the consumption of petroleum products. Traffic demand is the driving force of transportation energy consumption, and studying the influencing factors behind road traffic demand is crucial to alleviating the air pollution caused by transportation.

Some scholars have analyzed traffic demand from the perspective of elasticity. Musso et al. (2013) discussed the influence of rising fuel prices on road traffic demand from the perspective of price elasticity when the Greek government planned to raise fuel duties to 82 per cent in order to restore the budget surplus.

They pointed out that an increase in traffic demand would result in traffic congestion and then worsen air pollution. CO_2 discharge would also increase. Domestic and foreign scholars have made a number of empirical studies on the influencing factors of traffic demand. Wadud, Graham and Noland (2009) analyzed the relationship between highway capacity and road traffic demand and proposed that 25 per cent of the increase in road traffic demand, measured in vehicle kilometers (VKT), is attributable to enhancing highway capacity. Goodwin et al. (2004) and Tillema et al. (2013) held that the correlation between traffic demand and income is weakening. Graham and Glaister (2004), Goodwin et al. (2004) and Litman (2011) held that road traffic demand had an inelastic correlation with income. Sun et al. (2013) used panel data to analyze the relation between traffic demand and the spatial characteristics of a city and found that road density and the spatial scale of the city had a positive impact on traffic demand, while population density in the city and traffic congestion have negative impacts. Paulley et al. (2006) analyzed the relationship between traffic demand and traffic cost. Bresson et al. (2004) held that income is in negative correlation with public transport demand but has a positive correlation with private traffic demand. Orturzar et al. (2006) pointed out that economic growth promotes car ownership. Dargay and Gately (1997) pointed out that the faster the economic development of a country is, the closer the relationship between car ownership ratio and per capita income will be.

2.2 Model

Based on the existing research we summarized on road traffic demand, this chapter will analyze the three major influencing factors that affect traffic demand – transportation costs, transport infrastructure and economic activities – and establish a related conceptual model that shows the interaction between factors; a second structural equation model analyzes the relationship between traffic demand and factors of influence.

2.2.1 Conceptual model

Traffic cost $\Rightarrow$ traffic demand. When transportation costs increase, the traffic demand decreases. Goodwin (1995) and Litman (2011) point out that transportation costs associated with traffic demand is negative: when transportation cost is reduced, traffic demand increases. Although traffic demand causes traffic congestion, which would increase the cost of transportation, in the long term, this chapter assumes that, when traffic demand increases, improvements in transportation infrastructure will increase to meet the demand.

Transportation infrastructure $\Leftrightarrow$ traffic demand. Transportation infrastructure and transportation demand are in a two-way causal relationship, when traffic infrastructure stimulates traffic demand and produces the induced demand (such as Goodwin, 1995), and often when traffic demand increases, transportation infrastructure development will be promoted, such as roads to accommodate increased demand, as shown by Hansen and Huang (1997), who found that highway traffic demand is closely related to the highway mileage of two-stage or four-stage lag.

Economic activity ⇒ traffic demand. Economic activity is the fundamental cause of traffic demand, and an increase economic activity increases traffic demand, a positive correlation. Schafer (1998) is pointed out that increases in traffic volume can be attributed to GDP growth, while Atack et al. (2010) and Litman (2011) pointed out that economic development can promote traffic volume increase.

Transportation infrastructure ⇒ traffic cost. Transport infrastructure can be regarded as traffic supply. Considered from a more general supply and demand curve, when supply rises, prices decrease, and here, traffic infrastructure and transport costs have a negative correlation.

Economic activity ⇔ transportation infrastructure. Constructing transport infrastructure can help a country's productivity and employment. Novak et al. (1998) pointed out that the construction of transport infrastructure has the economic effects of increased employment, economic multipliers and enhanced national productivity and competitiveness.

Traffic cost ⇒ economic activity. Rising transportation costs will have a negative impact on economic activity.

2.2.2 Bayesian structural equation models

A structural equation model is a fusion of factor analysis and path analysis using multivariate statistical techniques and can be applied to multivariate quantitative study of the interaction relationship between variables. A basic structural equation model is divided into structural equation and measurement equation; among them, the measurement equation is used to indicate potential variables and the relationship between the observation indexes, while the structural equation captures the relationship between potential endogenous and exogenous variables.

2.2.3 Measurement equation

The measurement equation, using a confirmatory factor analysis model, is used to contact potential and corresponding observed variables (explicit index). Considering the error of measurement, this equation follows a regression model, taking observable variables and returning a lesser number of latent variables. Equation 2.1 is the measurement equation we will use.

$$y_i = \Lambda \omega_i + \varepsilon_i, i = 1,...,n \tag{2.1}$$

2.2.4 Structural equation

The structural equation is a return to class, with potential endogenous variables and several endogenous and exogenous latent variables of linear regression. Equation 2.2 is the structural equation we will use.

$$\eta_i = \Pi \eta_i + \Gamma \varsigma_i + \delta_i, i = 1,...,n \tag{2.2}$$

2.2.5 *The Bayesian estimation of SEM*

The fundamental statistical analysis of the structural equation model is usually adopted to establish, on the basis of the sample covariance matrix S of generalized least square method, the maximum likelihood method in Bayesian method. The results of the analysis depends on the sample covariance matrix S asymptotic distribution, but these methods all need to assume independent, identically distributed random values in the multivariate normal distribution. Without setting up some hypothesis, it is difficult to derive the sample covariance matrix and its asymptotic properties. And a Bayesian method of original observations, rather than the sample covariance matrix, or a Bayesian method based on sampling less dependent on asymptotic theory, even with a small sample situation, are likely to get reliable results.

2.3 Empirical analysis

Because of data availability, this chapter uses 2000–2012 transport demand data from China and 1990–2012 transport demand data from the US, divided into freight transportation demand and passenger transport demand. Using traffic volume (cargo weight or passengers) and transportation distance, including the flow of traffic demand and the process of two elements, this chapter measures traffic demand through a traffic turnover index. Using a structural equation model to analyze traffic demand factors involves the indicators shown in Table 2.1.

2.3.1 *Parameter estimation of structural equation model*

Equation 2.3 is the measurement equation we will use.

$$y_i = \Lambda \omega_i + \varepsilon_i, \tag{2.3}$$

Table 2.1 The potential variables corresponding observation index

Potential variables	Observations in China
Traffic demand (η)	Highway passenger turnover
	Volume of highway freight
Transportation infrastructure (ξ_1)	Highway mileage
	Urban per capita road area
	Number of vehicles (per km road)
Traffic cost (ξ_2)	Traffic class consumer price index
	Transport the consumer price index
	Vehicle fuel and spare parts the consumer price index
Economy activity (ξ_3)	GDP
	Per capita disposable income of urban households
	The proportion of urban residents

Where $\omega_i = (\eta_i, \xi_{i1}, \xi_{i2}, \xi_{i3})^T$, ε_i submit to $N[0, \Psi_\varepsilon]$ and use Equation 2.4.

$$\Lambda^T = \begin{pmatrix} 1 & \lambda_{2,1} & 0 & 0 & 0 & 0 & 0 & 0 & 0 & 0 & 0 \\ 0 & 0 & 1 & \lambda_{4,2} & \lambda_{5,2} & 0 & 0 & 0 & 0 & 0 & 0 \\ 0 & 0 & 0 & 0 & 0 & 1 & \lambda_{7,3} & \lambda_{8,3} & 0 & 0 & 0 \\ 0 & 0 & 0 & 0 & 0 & 0 & 0 & 0 & 1 & \lambda_{10,4} & \lambda_{11,4} \end{pmatrix} \quad (2.4)$$

Equation 2.5 is the structural equation we will use.

$$\eta_i = \gamma_1 \xi_1 + \gamma_2 \xi_2 + \gamma_3 \xi_3 + \delta \quad (2.5)$$

Where $(\xi_1, \xi_2, \xi_3)^T$ and σ independent distributed in $N[0, \Phi]$ and $N[0, \Psi_\delta]$.

Bayesian analysis was carried out on the structural equation model in Equation 2.5; the conjugate prior distribution was carried out using Equation 2.6.

$$\Phi^{-1} \overset{D}{=} W_3[B,10]; \psi_{\varepsilon k}^{-1} \overset{D}{=} Gamma[6,10]; \Lambda_k \overset{D}{=} N[0.8, 4\psi_{\omega k}I];$$

$$\psi_\delta^{-1} \overset{D}{=} Gamma[6,10]; \Gamma \overset{D}{=} N[M, \psi_\delta I]; \quad (2.6)$$

$$B = \begin{pmatrix} 2 & -1 & 0 \\ -1 & 2 & -1 \\ 0 & -1 & 2 \end{pmatrix}; M = \begin{pmatrix} 0.5 \\ -0.5 \\ 0.5 \end{pmatrix}$$

Where I is the units of the corresponding dimension matrix.

Using WinBUGS software, we performed standardized data processing in the Bayesian estimation structural equation model. As shown in Figure 2.1, we used different initial values as the parameter in the sequence diagram, resulting in an algorithm convergence within 1,000 iterations. For parameter estimation, this chapter discards the previous 2,000 iterations and uses the convergence of $T* = 8,000$ samples until Bayesian estimation results are obtained.

The results of parameter estimation of the Chinese and American road traffic demand structural models obtained by WinBUGS are shown in Figure 2.2, where we can see that the direct impact effect on traffic demand is that the both countries' economic activity have the greatest impact on their traffic demand and that the coefficients are 0.64 and 0.69, respectively. Also, we can see the impact of transport infrastructure on traffic demand, and the direct influence coefficients in China and US are 0.62 and 0.64 respectively. The influence of transportation cost on traffic demand is minimum and negative, coefficients are –0.58 and –0.43 respectively. Second, we consider the indirect impact of the traffic infrastructure that through the transport costs and economic activities on the road traffic demand. The size of the indirect influence is measured by the product of

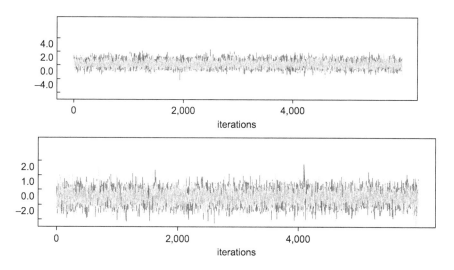

Figure 2.1 λ7, 3, γ2 under three different initial values of parameters of the sequence diagram

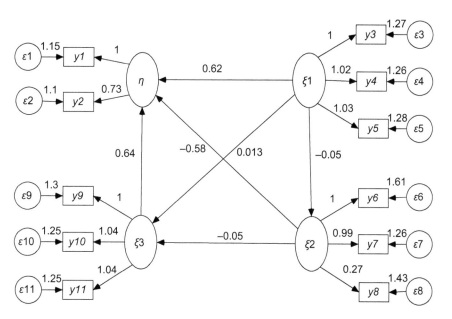

Figure 2.2 The Bayesian estimation of a structural equation model of China traffic demand

the covariance between the latent variables and the direct influence coefficient. The indirect effect of the traffic infrastructure on the traffic demand are 0.04 and 0.08, where the indirect effect of the traffic cost is 0.03 and 0.004, and the indirect effects of economic activity are 0.01 and 0.076. The indirect impact of traffic costs on traffic demand through economic activity is –0.03 and –0.03 respectively. Third, we consider the comprehensive effect, which is the combination of the direct effect and the indirect effect. We find that the comprehensive effect of the available traffic infrastructure is 0.66 and 0.72; the comprehensive effect of economic activity is 0.64 and 0 .69; and the combined effect of traffic cost is –0.61 and –0.46. Thus, while the indirect influence of the interaction between latent variables is taken into account, the traffic infrastructure becomes the most important factor of road traffic demand.

2.4 Conclusion

In analyzing the influencing factors of road traffic demand, China and the United States have shown that the direct impact of economic activity is the largest, followed by the transport infrastructure, and the direct impact of transport cost is the smallest. When considering the interaction between latent variables and indirect effects, the biggest comprehensive effect is traffic infrastructure, followed by economic activity; the comprehensive effect of transportation costs on road traffic demand still the smallest. While road traffic demand is an influencing factor in both China and the United States, the main difference between the two countries is that the influence of transportation costs on road traffic demand in the US is significantly less than in China. Chinese consumers are more sensitive to transportation costs than American consumers, mainly due to relative per capita income and higher transportation and fuel prices in China.

Compared with passenger demand, cargo demand is more sensitive to price. In China's case, diesel demand has an asymmetrical effect on both passenger and cargo, while changes in gasoline prices only has an asymmetrical effect on passenger transport demand. In the US, changes in gasoline and diesel prices have asymmetrical effects on passenger and cargo. China's gasoline and diesel prices are among the highest, and traffic demand is positively related to historical prices: when prices exceed the previous highest price, traffic demand continues to rise as well because oil prices in China have followed a "rise more, fall less" pattern for a long time, giving consumers irrational expectations.

3 Analysis of road transport energy consumption demand in China

In this chapter, we will first analyze historical trends in total transportation industry turnover relative to GDP in typical economies. The two indexes present obvious "Inverted L" type patterns. Then, we will explore the potential relationship between total road transportation turnover and GDP and the associated energy consumption because total turnover and GDP are important factors in road transport energy consumption. Next, we employ path analysis to analyze the impact mechanism of factors related to road transport energy consumption. We will adopt the Bayesian model average (BMA) model to select core factors related to road transport energy consumption in China, and on the basis of the model selection as well as univariate models (Exponential Smoothing Technology (ETS) and Autoregressive Integrated Moving Average (ARIMA) models) and multivariate (multiple regression) models, we will analyze and forecast road transport energy consumption. Our results show that road transport energy consumption rises by 0.33 per cent for every per cent increase in GDP and by 1.26 percentage points for every per cent increase in urbanization. Road transport energy consumption in China reached around 226,181.1 kilotons (kt) of oil equivalent by the end of 2015 and is expected to reach about 379,069 kt of oil equivalent by 2021.

3.1 Introduction

Transportation plays an important support role for both social development and national economic development. With China's rapid economic development, industrialization and accelerated urbanization, transportation demand has also been increasing and its share of the total energy consumption in the economy has also been proportionally rising. At present, transportation industry energy consumption accounts for about 9 per cent of China's total energy consumption, and this proportion is increasing. In the 1990s, China's transport energy consumption increased from 2180 kt of oil equivalent to 58027.99 kt of oil equivalent (World Bank, Carbon Dioxide Information Analysis Center (n.d.)). Entering the twenty-first century, China's transportation energy consumption accelerated significantly with an average annual growth rate of 9.8 per cent from 2000 to 2008 (*China Statistical Yearbook* 2008). From the structure of the transport sector's energy consumption, road transport can be seen as the major energy consuming subsector. The China Energy Research Association (www.cers.org. cn/) estimated that, in 1990, 1995 and 2000, road transport energy consumption accounted for 47.6 per cent, 59 per cent and 68.1 per cent respectively of total transportation energy consumption. The transportation industry is one of the primary contributors to greenhouse gases and other polluting emissions, with vehicle pollution progressively becoming the main source of pollution in big cities. Thus, controlling these emissions constitutes a major challenge for carbon emissions control efforts. According to the World Health Organization (n.d.), atmospheric pollutants from motor vehicle emissions account for about 30 per cent of the total emissions in some big cities at present; a large part of PM2.5 in the air is composed of automobile tail gas discharges.

As economic transformation and the development of the Chinese economy are set to continue, the transportation industry is expected to also change and acquire new characteristics. Following a period of mid- and high-speed economic growth, transportation production is also expected to grow at a mid/high speed of about 5–7 per cent. In 2014, railways, highways, waterways and civil aviation passenger traffic growth were expected to be about 3.7 per cent, and freight volume growth, about 7.2 per cent (China National Bureau of Statistics, *China Statistical Yearbook*, 2014). Due to the downward pressure on the economy, as well as the natural resource and environmental constraints, the sustainable development of the transportation industry is facing severe challenges. Therefore, an analysis of China's road transport energy consumption demand is of great significance in this "new normal" period.

Transportation energy consumption has become a very important issue and is receiving increasing attention around the world. Considering the scarcity of natural resources and the increasing energy demand, an analysis of transportation energy consumption and an examination into consumption and the associated emissions reductions has practical significance. Anable et al. (2012) insisted that social energy consumption and associated emissions were affected by technical efficiency, lifestyles and social and cultural factors. Based on this categorization, they used an integrated suite of sectorial and whole system models to explore potential energy pathways in the UK transport sector. The results showed that social energy utilization and environmental and health factors could change energy utilization and reduce emissions. Al-Ghandoor et al. (2013) analyzed gasoline consumption in the Jordanian traffic industry by establishing a multiple regression model to determine the main factors affecting transportation energy demand, which were identified to be the number of vehicle registrations, income levels and the price of gasoline. Chi et al. (2012) examined the demand for air travel in the US by establishing a function between actual income, air transport price and aviation demand. Their results showed that there was a long-term equilibrium relationship between these three aspects, with income being the airline industry's long-term decision factor. Yan and Crookes (2010) summarized China's traffic energy consumption and energy saving potential from a lifecycle perspective through an analysis of the Chinese road transportation industry in terms of vehicle ownership, infrastructure, energy usage, carbon emissions and other related situations. Wang et al. (2014) discussed and analyzed the status of the Chinese transportation industry and the energy consumption growth trends for four different modes of transport: roads, railways, waterways and civil aviation. They also put forward several political suggestions by analyzing the main technical obstacles and addressing policy issues for energy savings in the Chinese transportation industry. Wang and Lu (2014) selected carriage of goods data from 31 provinces and cities in China to measure the rebound effect in the short and long term using a double logarithmic regression equation and an error correction model. The results showed that, in the long term, the partial rebound effect for road freight transportation was 84 per cent for the whole nation, which can be broken down to 52 per cent, 80 per cent and 78 per cent for the eastern, central and western regions in China respectively. In the short term, a tiny super-conservation effect was found in Chinese road freight transportation. Shunping et al. (2010) analyzed the differences between transportation energy consumption in China and in the world and concluded that China's current statistics lacked energy consumption data for social and private cars, motorcycles, low-speed automobiles and agricultural automobiles. They established an energy consumption transportation model and calculated the related parameters based on vehicle usage. They then compared China's transportation energy consumption level with other developed countries and found that China's per capita energy consumption and transportation energy consumption proportion were relatively low but had increased in recent years. Sun et al. (2013) analyzed China's urban traffic structure and maintained that vehicle numbers, fuel consumption per 100 kilometers and annual mileage were the main factors exerting influence on urban transportation energy consumption. They introduced a rate of change as parameters into the influencing factors and, using a logarithmic mean Divisia index (LMDI) model, established an urban transportation energy consumption dynamic scene combinational decomposition model. According to changes in these 3 factors, they established a 12-scenario model and analyzed urban traffic energy consumption trends under different modes. Zhang et al. (2006) established a transportation energy consumption decomposition model to analyze the contribution of traffic service level, transportation mode shares and energy consumption intensity to transport energy consumption from 1980 to 2001. Their results showed that transportation service turnover was the main driving force behind energy consumption, while changes in transportation structure exacerbated the growth. A reduction in energy intensity in the past was not enough to prevent an increase in energy consumption. However, as energy intensity has been increasing in recent years, they concluded that growth in transportation oil consumption is inevitable.

In summarizing the findings of previous studies, some driving factors in road transport energy consumption demand are apparent. Economic development boosts the growth of road transportation total turnover, which increases road transport energy consumption. However, improvements in energy efficiency can reduce road transport energy consumption and pollutant emissions. Gasoline prices and national fuel tax policy changes also affect road transport energy consumption to a certain extent. With the promotion of an energy conservation and emissions reduction policy, the contradictions between employment, energy conservation and emissions reduction are sharpening. The government needs to be able to ensure the employment rate as a precondition for meeting the energy conservation and emissions reduction targets and consider the positive interactive relationships between economic developments, employment and emissions reduction in an integrated manner. Many scholars have examined the potential relationship between energy consumption and employment using the CGE model. They put policy, economic growth, employment, energy consumption and environmental impact into the system and researched the interactive relationships (Allan et al., 2007; Hanley et al., 2009) found that road transport energy consumption was affected by both market conditions and government policies. However, few articles have considered financial credit and employment as factors which may affect road transport energy consumption in China. Much previous research has predicted transport energy consumption using traditional analysis methods, such as simple linear regressions and double logarithmic models. These models, however, are unable to effectively analyze the promotion and constraining factors; consequently, parameter estimation errors occur.

As one of the most important infrastructure developments, the transportation industry is based on energy and promotes development. As economies develop, transportation demand increases, but the current focus on energy saving and emissions reduction policies highlights the contradiction between transportation development and energy demand. Because of this, we chose road transport as our research objective, as this sector has the largest proportion of transport energy consumption. Based on the literature review, and including Chinese and foreign research results, we first analyzed the historical total road turnover and GDP trends in the United States, Japan, the European Union and China while exploring the potential relationships between total road turnover, GDP and road energy consumption, as both total turnover and GDP are considered influencing factors for road transport energy consumption. Then, we employed a path analysis method to analyze the impact mechanism of the factors related to road transport energy consumption and selected total road turnover, highway mileage, GDP, population, urbanization rate, automobile industry output, automobile credit, core business taxes, extra car manufacturing charges and the average number of automobile manufacturing employees as factors, under consideration of the supply, demand, cost, technological progress and national policy. We adopted a Bayesian model averaging method to select the core factors related to road transport energy consumption in China. On the basis of model selection as well as univariate (ETS and ARIMA models) and multivariate (multiple regression) models, road transport energy consumption was analyzed and forecast.

3.2 Methods

In order to analyze road transport energy consumption, we need to first analyze influential factors. In 1921, the population geneticist Sewall Wright proposed path analysis, which was a continuation of simple correlation analysis. From multiple regressions, a correlation coefficient is derived, and the direct effect of the variables on the dependent variables as well as on the indirect and combined effects of other variables on the dependent variables can be expressed using a direct path, an indirect path and a total path coefficient. Chai et al. (2011) used this method to analyze the influential factors for oil prices.

3.2.1 Path analysis model

The standardized multiple linear regression model can be obtained from Equation 3.1.

$$y = \beta_0 + \beta_1 x_1 + \beta_2 x_2 + \cdots + \beta_k x_k \tag{3.1}$$

Where the independent variables are $x_1, x_2, \ldots, x_k$ and the dependent variable is y.

Suppose σ_y is the sample standard deviation of y and σ_x is the sample standard deviation of x_i. Then, let $\beta_i' = \beta_i \dfrac{\sigma_{x_i}}{\sigma_y}$, β_i' be the standardized coefficient.

It can be seen that this standardized coefficient is correlated, not only with the independent variable regression coefficients, but also with the volatility of the independent variables. If the volatility (standard deviation of the independent variables) is large, the independent variable becomes more important; otherwise, the variable is less important. However, when using this formula to solve standardized coefficients, any interactions between the variables or the impact of the other variables are not considered. However, using a path analysis method, this problem can be easily solved.

The decomposition equation for the simple correlation coefficients can be expressed as in Equation 3.2.

$$\begin{cases} p_{1y} + r_{12}p_{2y} + \cdots + r_{1k}p_{ky} = r_{1y} \\ r_{21}p_{1y} + p_{2y} + \cdots + r_{2k}p_{ky} = r_{2y} \\ \quad \cdots \\ r_{k1}p_{1y} + r_{k2}p_{2y} + \cdots + p_{ky} = r_{ky} \end{cases} \tag{3.2}$$

Where r_{ij} stands for the simple correlation coefficients for x_i and x_j, and r_{ij} stands for the simple correlation coefficients for x_i and y. This is a basic path analysis model where p_{iy} is a direct path, the partial correlation coefficient of x_i and y after standardization, and indicates the direct effect of x_i on y. The direct coefficient of determination is $R_i^2 = p_{iy}^2$; $r_{ij}p_{jy}$, the indirect path, and indicates the indirect influence of x_i on y through x_j. $R_{ij}^2 = 2p_{iy}r_{ij}p_{jy}$ is the indirect coefficient of determination, and $R(i)^2 = R_i^2 + \sum_{i \neq j} R_{ij}^2$ indicates the combined influence of x_i

on y and is called the *decision coefficient*. $\sum\limits_{i \neq j} r_{ij} p_{jy}$ indicates the total indirect effect of x_i on the independent variable through all the other variables. These equations are used to decompose the simple correlation coefficient for each independent variable and dependent variable into p_{iy} (direct path effect) and $\sum\limits_{i \neq j} r_{ij} p_{jy}$ (total indirect path effect). Because of the complex interactions between economic phenomena, it is impossible to take all factors into account when building the model. Therefore, it is important to further calculate the path effect coefficient for the omitted variables and errors on the dependent variable, that is the *residual effect*, p_{ay}. The computational formula is $p_{ay} = \sqrt{1 - \sum\limits_{i=1}^{k} p_{iy} r_{iy}}$. If the residual effect is small, the path analysis has successfully grasped the main variables; otherwise, the path analysis may be missing some main factors, meaning that other factors are needed in the analysis.

Path analysis is not an ordinary standard multiple linear regression analysis as it is not used to predict and control. Nor is it a correlation analysis because the path coefficients are vectors; if x_i and y are swapped, $p_{iy} \neq p_{yi}$, and the path coefficient values can be greater than 1 or less than –1 in real numbers. The purpose of path analysis is to decompose the correlation coefficients of the independent variable x_i and the dependent variable y into a direct effect p_{iy} and an indirect effect $r_{iy} p_{iy}$. This tells us the following: first, p_{iy} indicates the intrinsic effect of x_i on y, without considering the influence of other variables; second, in the complex correlations between several variables x_1, x_2, . . ., x_k y and r_{iy} are unable to describe the full relationship between x_i and y as there are indirect effects; third, it is meaningful for decision-makers to find the independent variable paths of influence on y from these complex multiple correlations.

To a certain extent, transportation infrastructure reflects a country's level of economic development. Substantial growth in highway energy consumption is the most direct reason for the increase in highway transportation demand, and the main reason for the increasing demand is economic development and social progress. However, the relationship between the economy and transportation is not a simple linear relationship. Therefore, the characteristics of the relationship between social development and transportation demand are the premise for analyzing road energy demand. This chapter seeks to compare total road turnover with GDP in developed economies to determine the road traffic characteristics in developed economics. Based on these findings, we then analyze the current developments in China's road traffic and infer future development trends.

3.2.2 The relational characteristics between total road turnover and GDP in developed economies

At different stages, road transport energy demand in each economy has followed different patterns. Depending upon the status of the country's transport infrastructure, accessibility of data and the developed economy's features, we selected the United States, Japan, the Netherlands, Germany and the European Union as the analysis objects (Data sources: World Bank, Carbon Dioxide Information Analysis Center (n.d.) for China: 1960–2013; Japan: 1983–2009; United States: 1990–2009; the Netherlands: 1990–2011; Germany: 2000–2011; EU: 1995–2009). The European Union's 27 trend lines are listed separately as the World Bank and Eurostat statistics were different (Figures 3.1 and 3.2).

Figures 3.1 and 3.2 illustrate historical total road turnover and GDP trends as an obvious "Inverted L" type pattern (logarithmic curve) in these typical economies. As different economies have different populations, the logarithmic growth is different. Overall, the total road turnover tends to a stable state after a period of high growth. The regression fitting degree (Table 3.1) shows that the

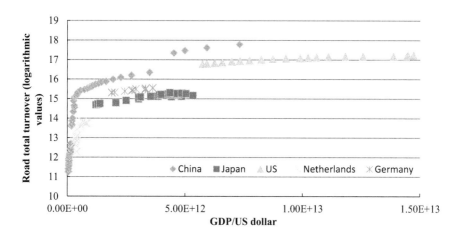

Figure 3.1 Total road turnover trends (logarithmic values) and GDP for China, Japan, America, Germany and Holland

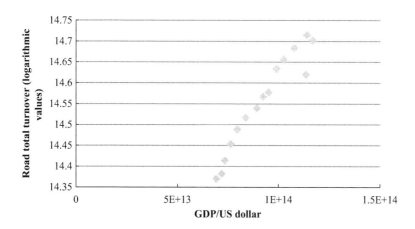

Figure 3.2 Total road turnover trends (logarithmic values) and GDP for the UN

Table 3.1 The trend fitting functions for total road turnover and the GDP in developed economies

	Fitting functions	R^2
China	$y = 1.323\ln(x) - 21.05$	0.923
America	$y = 0.456\ln(x) + 3.420$	0.949
Japan	$y = 0.412\ln(x) + 3.208$	0.894
Germany	$y = 0.355\ln(x) + 5.246$	0.942
Netherlands	$y = 1.208\ln(x) - 19.32$	0.706
European Union	$y = 0.630\ln(x) - 5.707$	0.951

United States and Japan have 95 per cent and 89 per cent traffic development respectively and China's is also high at 92 per cent. As the largest developing country, China road traffic construction is not yet perfect with transport links being at the same level as in the United States in the 1980s. Since China's motor vehicle penetration rate is low compared with the developed countries, public transportation development and transportation in general is relatively concentrated, and total road traffic turnover is mainly affected by GDP, urbanization and industrialization. With China's rapid economic development, industrialization and accelerated urbanization, transportation demand is also increasing. After industrialization, developed countries began to reverse the urbanization process. At the same time, vehicle utilization increased gradually and the contribution rate of road turnover to GDP decreased accordingly. Hence, the relationship between total road traffic turnover and GDP presents approximate logarithmic growth trends. However, China's transportation energy consumption intensity is still very low. In 2007, China's transportation energy consumption intensity was 0.012 kgoe/$PPP, which was only 36 per cent of the global average, 24 per cent of that in the United States, 43 per cent of that in the European Union and 55 per cent of that in Japan. As private car ownership and total road turnover increase, a decline in China's transport energy consumption is unlikely and is expected to rise. However, at present, automobile fuel efficiency in China is comparable to the developed world, but the two important factors causing China's high energy consumption are the preference for SUVs over ordinary cars and the many older, less fuel-efficient cars still being used.

The trend analysis in Table 3.1 shows that total turnover and GDP have an obvious "Inverted L" relationship and that road total turnover and GDP are both important contributing factors to road transport energy demand. Therefore, these two factors and energy consumption do not constitute a simple pair of influence as there is a significant interaction effect between the three factors, which indicates that there is a significant effect on the relationship between the three factors. To further illustrate the intrinsic linkages between these three indexes, we used path analysis for further research (Table 3.2).

All three correlations (between total road turnover, GDP and road transport energy consumption) have remained at around 95 per cent. The correlation between GDP and road transport energy consumption is the largest at about

Table 3.2 Path analysis for the effect of total turnover and GDP on aviation fuel
efficiency

Independent variable	Combined action	Direct action	Indirect action	Decision coefficient	T-test
Total turnover	0.9484	0.0350	0.9134	0.0652	0.4446
GDP	0.9896	0.9561	0.0335	0.9782	12.1351

98 per cent. We can see from Table 3.1 that total road turnover did not obviously pass the T-test, which indicates that there are multicollinear relationships between total road turnover and GDP. Because total road turnover reflects road transport demand under economic development, it also includes economic impact. The direct effect (in absolute values) and the combined size sorting effects (in absolute values for the correlation coefficients) are GDP > RTT. We can see that GDP has the most significant effect on China's road transport energy consumption from direct as well as combined effects. The decision effect factor coefficients can be calculated as: $R(TT)^2 = 0.0652$, $R(GDP)^2 = 0.9782$. Therefore, total road turnover and GDP are the main push factors for road transport energy consumption, and the GDP-promoting function is greater than the total road turnover. The determination coefficient $R^2 = \sum_{i=1}^{3} p_{iy} r_{iy} = 0.8564$ expresses the interpretation capacity of the selected factors for the dependent variable. That is to say, the path analysis does not cover the primary effect factors, i.e. some factors are not considered. Therefore, we need to further analyze the other influential factors affecting road energy demand to determine all the core influencing factors.

3.2.3 Influencing factors for road energy consumption

The factors that affect road transport energy consumption can be generally divided into the market and the government. Economic development results in road transportation demand growth, which in turn results in increasing road transport energy consumption. An increased energy utilization rate can reduce road transportation energy consumption and pollutant emissions, as can the price of gasoline and national fuel tax policy changes. At the same time, with continual energy saving emissions reduction policies, contradictions between employment and reductions become increasingly serious. The government has to simultaneously consider economic development, employment and energy savings and emissions reduction and cannot simply achieve emissions reduction targets at the cost of GDP and employment. Therefore, here, we consider the influential factors for road transport energy consumption from the perspective of demand, supply, cost and national policy. We used the following data sources: WIND database, World Bank, and *Chinese Statistical Yearbook* annual data for energy consumption, GDP, highway mileage, total road turnover, population and urbanization rate (1971–2011); for output of automobile industry (1992–2011); for automobile credit (2001–2011); for core business taxes, extra automobile manufacturing charges and the average number of employees in the automobile manufacturing industry (1999–2011).

Economic development

Since reform and opening up, the Chinese economy has experienced sustained rapid development for 30 years. This has been especially evident since entering the industrialization stage in 2000, since which the Chinese GDP growth rate has been maintained at around 8 per cent. From 1978 to 2010, however, China's annual average GDP growth rate was 9.9 per cent. In 2013, China's GDP was 9.18 trillion dollars with an actual growth rate of about 7.8 per cent, ranking it the second largest economy in the world. However, because of the influence of the demographic dividend and a series of other factors, current economic growth has reached a "new normal", which means that economic growth has entered a mid- to high-speed growth period. The economic growth rate is expected to drop from 10 per cent over the past 30 years to around 6–8 per cent in the coming decade. In the "new normal", road traffic development is expected to also enter a new stage. Through a simple linear regression equation (Equation 3.3), we can see that road transport energy consumption rises by 0.58 per cent for every percentage point growth in GDP. The fitting degree of the equation is 97.87 per cent (Table 3.3).

$$\ln y = 0.58 \ln GDP + 4.23 \qquad (3.3)$$

Demand and supply

There are two factors affecting road energy consumption demand. The first is that highway mileage affects road transport demand through the impact of road transport direct demand, and the second is that total road turnover by socio-economic development influences road energy consumption demand. Highway mileage could be considered a supply factor that meets traffic demand, while total road turnover is a reflection of road traffic consumption under socio-economic development. In other words, these two are demand factors. To avoid multicollinearity between highway mileage and total turnover, we will use a path analysis method.

Table 3.3 OLS regression results for GDP on road transport energy consumption

Variable	Coefficient	Std. Error	t-Statistic	Prob.
GDP	0.584144	0.013623	42.87998	0.0000
C	4.233105	0.140355	30.15991	0.0000

Table 3.4 Path analysis for the effect of total turnover and highway kilometers on road transport energy consumption

Independent variable	Combined action	Direct action	Indirect action	Decision coefficient	T-test
Total turnover	0.9484	0.5297	0.4187	0.7242	8.1538
Highway mileage	0.9423	0.4848	0.4575	0.6786	7.4625

Table 3.5 OLS regression results for total turnover and highway mileage on road transport energy consumption

Variable	Coefficient	Std. error	t-Statistic	Prob.
RTT	0.340915	0.041989	8.119081	0.0000
HM	0.901842	0.121355	7.431421	0.0000
C	2.294816	0.309566	7.413009	0.0000

We can see from Table 3.4 that total road turnover and highway mileage pass the T-test, which indicates there is no multicollinearity between total road turnover and highway mileage. The direct effect (in absolute values) and the combined effect (in absolute values for the correlation coefficients) size sorting is road turnover (RTT) > highway mileage (HM). No matter whether a direct effect or a combined effect, we find that total road turnover has the most significant effect on China's road energy consumption. The decision coefficient for the effect factors can be calculated as: $R(RTT)^2 = 0.7242$, $R(HM)^2 = 0.6786$. Therefore, total road turnover (RTT) and highway mileage (HM) are the main push factors for road transport energy consumption, and the promoting function for total road turnover is greater than that for highway mileage. The determination coefficient $R^2 = \sum_{i=1}^{3} p_{iy} r_{iy} = 0.7981$ expresses the interpretation capacity of the selected factors for the dependent variable, which is 79.81 per cent. This means that the path analysis does not cover the primary effect factors as some factors have not been considered. We continued the simple linear regression to measure the elastic coefficient for total road turnover and highway mileage (Table 3.5). The findings showed that road transport energy consumption rises by 0.34 per cent for each per cent rise in total road turnover, and by 0.9 per cent for each per cent rise in highway mileage. Using Equation 3.4, the fitting degree is 95.67 per cent.

$$\ln y = 0.34 \ln RTT + 0.90 \ln HM + 2.29 \qquad (3.4)$$

Population scale

Much previous research has shown that population size and urbanization are core energy consumption driving factors and that the urban population driving force proportion has become greater than population size. Zhou et al. (2012) and Liu (2009) examined the correlation between energy consumption and urbanization and found a one-way Granger causality relationship between urbanization and energy consumption in China in both the short and the long term.

Table 3.6 shows that population does not pass the T-test, which indicates that multicollinearity exists between population and the urbanization rate. The population index is therefore removed. The direct effect (in absolute values), and the combined effect (in absolute values for the correlation coefficient) size sorting, is Urban > P. No matter whether a direct effect or combined effect, it is obvious that urbanization has a significant effect on China's road energy consumption. Urbanization growth acceleration leads to increased transportation and infrastructure, which is eventually reflected in the transport energy demand. The driving force of the urban population proportion has become greater than overall population size. The decision effect factor coefficients can be calculated as: $R(P)^2 = 0.1917$, $R(Urban)^2 = 0.9670$. Therefore, urbanization and population are the main push factors for road transport energy consumption, with urbanization creating greater demand for road transportation than population growth. The determination coefficient $R^2 = \sum_{i=1}^{3} p_{iy}r_{iy} = 0.8519$ expresses the interpretation capacity of the selected factors as the dependent variable reaches 85.19 per cent. This means that the path analysis does not cover the primary effect factors, i.e. some factors are not considered. The linear regression findings show that road transport energy consumption rises by 2.83 per cent for every 1 percentage point increase in urbanization (Table 3.7). Using Equation 3.5, the fitting degree is 97.65 per cent.

$$\ln y = 2.83 \ln Urban + 0.77 \tag{3.5}$$

Table 3.6 Path analysis for the effect of population and urbanization rate on road transport energy consumption

Independent variable	Combined action	Direct action	Indirect action	Decision coefficient	T-test
Population	0.9638	0.1052	0.8586	0.1917	1.0947
Urbanization rate	0.9886	0.8868	0.1019	0.9670	9.2279

Table 3.7 OLS regression results for urbanization rate on road transport energy consumption

Variable	Coefficient	Std. error	t-Statistic	Prob.
Urban	2.827322	0.069260	40.82170	0.0000
C	0.771951	0.231477	3.334888	0.0019

Credit financing

China's automobile consumption credit market started relatively late. Since 2003, the automobile credit industry has matured, and the average annual growth rate has held steady at 5–8 per cent. With the development of the financial credit disbursed to automobile users, demand is increasing, which in turn has led to an increase in road transport energy consumption. We selected auto credit, core business taxes and extra automobile manufacturing charges as indexes of credit financing.

Table 3.8 shows that automobile credit does not pass the T-test, which indicates that there is multicollinearity in the relationship between automobile credits (Credit), core business taxes and extra car manufacturing charges (CBT). At present, automobile credits are not a core influencing factor for road transport energy consumption. Because China's auto consumption credit started relatively late, core business taxes and extra car manufacturing charges have a direct reaction on auto industry development. The direct effect (in absolute values) and the combined effect (in absolute values for the correlation coefficient) size sorting is CBT > Credit. No matter whether a direct effect or a combined effect, core business taxes and the extra car manufacturing charges have a significant effect on China's road transport energy consumption. The effect factor decision coefficients can be calculated as: $R(Credit)^2 = -0.1403$, $R(CMBI)^2 = 0.9809$. Therefore, core business taxes and extra car manufacturing charges are the main push factors for road transport energy consumption, and automobile credit is a limiting factor for road transport consumption. The determination coefficient

$$R^2 = \sum_{i=1}^{3} p_{iy}r_{iy} = 0.8998$$ expresses the interpretation capacity of the selected fac-

tors for the dependent variable and reaches 89.98 per cent, indicating that some factors may not have been considered.

When we calculated the elasticity from data obtained from the *China Statistical Yearbook* from 1999 to 2011 (annual data), the degree of freedom was found to be lower. Within such models with greater uncertainty, a small sample assessment can cause large errors. Therefore, this chapter uses the Bayesian statistics technique, which is suitable for small sample conditions, to assess the regression model. With the assistance of WinBUGS software, the parameter estimation value for the simple regression analysis acts as the starting value for the relevant solve-for parameter in the Bayesian regression model. 10,000 iterations

Table 3.8 Path analysis for the effect of automobile credit, core business taxes and extra automobile manufacturing industry charges on road transport energy consumption

Independent variable	Combined action	Direct action	Indirect action	Decision coefficient	T-test
Automobile credit	0.6875	−0.0954	0.7829	−0.1403	−1.8227
CBT	0.9929	1.0631	−0.0703	0.9809	20.3078

were performed. The first 5,000 iterations acted as the test sample and the second 5,000 iterations acted as the assessment sample. With a prerequisite of fine convergence and normality, this chapter presents the assessment results for the two Bayesian regression models, as shown in Table 3.9. The elastic result of Equation 3.6 shows that road transport energy consumption rises by 0.41 per cent for each per cent rise in core business taxes and extra car manufacturing charges.

$$\ln y = 0.414 \ln CMBI + 5.387 \tag{3.6}$$

Automobile industry output

The development level of the auto industry is a symbol of transportation development. Therefore, auto industry output influences road transport consumption demand. According to the small sample, we also used the Bayesian regression model as earlier. Using Equation 3.7, the estimation results in Table 3.10 show that road transport energy consumption rises by 0.54 per cent for each per cent rise in auto industry output.

$$\ln y = 0.5424 \ln Output + 1.1400 \tag{3.7}$$

Automobile manufacturing: average number of all employees

China is still in an important stage of industrialization and urbanization and is faced with multiple target constraints in terms of economic growth stability, employment stability, pollution emissions reduction and others, and contradictions between employment, energy conservation and emissions reduction are sharpening. In the past ten years, the total number of employed has continued to increase, but the employment growth rate has been annually decreasing, and there is disproportionate growth in the labor force. Against this background,

Table 3.9 Bayesian regression results for automobile credit, core business taxes and extra automobile manufacturing industry charges on road transport energy consumption

	Mean	*Sd*	*MC_error*	*val2.5pc*	*Median*
CBT	0.414	0.1133	0.01284	0.2008	0.4065
C	5.387	1.649	0.1868	1.854	5.502

Table 3.10 Bayesian regression results for automobile industry output on road transport energy consumption

	Mean	*Sd*	*MC_error*	*val2.5pc*	*Median*
Output	0.5424	0.1393	0.01419	0.2175	0.5467
C	1.14	0.1161	4.668	6.625	9.326

Table 3.11 Bayesian regression results for core business taxes and extra automobile manufacturing industry charges on road transport energy consumption

	Mean	Sd	MC_error	val2.5pc	Median
Employment	1.029	0.1756	0.02049	0.7467	0.9742
C	−3.616	2.563	0.299	−8.166	−2.815

it is necessary to consider economic development, employment, energy saving and emissions reduction synergistically and not simply restrain GDP and the employment growth rate for emissions reduction. In this chapter, to consider the relationship between road transport energy consumption and employment, we selected the average number of automobile manufacturing employees as the influencing factor. According to the small sample, we also used the Bayesian regression model as earlier. Using Equation 3.8, the estimation results show that road transport energy consumption will rise by 1.03 per cent for each percentage point increase in automobile manufacturing employees (Table 3.11).

$$\ln y = 1.029 \ln Employment - 3.616 \qquad (3.8)$$

3.3 Results and discussion

Table 3.12 shows a review of the influencing factors' elasticity. The results showed that all these core factors were the main push factors for road transport energy consumption. Elasticity size sorting shows that the urbanization rate > average number of automobile manufacturing industry employees > highway mileage > GDP > auto industry output > auto manufacturing: main business taxes and surcharges > total road turnover. The urbanization rate was found to be the most elastic, followed by the average number of automobile manufacturing employees at more than 1 per cent. Road transport energy consumption was found to rise by 2.83 for each percentage point increase in urbanization but only by 1.03 per cent for each percentage point increase in the average number of automobile manufacturing employees. These results indicate that the urbanization rate is the main driving force affecting road transport energy consumption and conforms to China's current development situation. An acceleration in urbanization, followed by transportation and infrastructure, would be eventually reflected in transport energy demand. With the Chinese urbanization rate continuing to increase as more people move to the cities and towns from countryside, the consumption structure changes, traffic demand increases, and there is an increase on the construction of corresponding infrastructure. In conclusion, transportation is needed as a result of both population mobility and infrastructure.

The change in direction for employment and road transport energy consumption is the same. The realistic choice of industrial emissions is focused on strengthening governance and promoting technology to reduce emissions, while taking into account the structure of emissions reduction. The concrete measures in the automotive manufacturing industry are that the government reduces the demand for automobiles through relevant policies to encourage more people to

Table 3.12 The elasticity results for all core influencing factors

Independent variable	Elasticity
GDP	0.584
Total turnover	0.341
Highway mileage	0.902
Urbanization rate	2.827
CBT	0.414
Output	0.542
Employment	1.029

drive green, while the automobile manufacturers enhance the efficient alloca-
tion of resources by introducing mechanized production instead of maintaining
manual operations. As a result, employment and energy consumption will tend
to change in the same direction. When there are job losses, the demand for cars is
reduced, and road transport energy consumption is reduced accordingly. On the
contrary, if more jobs are offered, road transport energy consumption increases.
At the same time, China's auto manufacturing technological level is low compared with developed countries as most labor are production rather than skilled
workers; when a factory slows production, a large number of production workers
lose their jobs. Therefore, the elasticity coefficient of road transport energy consumption to automobile manufacturing employment exceeds 1.

The elasticity of the two demand factors is different. The elasticity of total road
turnover is a minimum for all factors. Road transport energy consumption rises
by 0.34 for each percentage point increase in total road turnover and by 0.9 per
cent in the case of highway mileage. This further illustrates that the total turnover
index is not only a reflection of road transportation demand but also includes
social and economic influences. Therefore, the elasticity of total road turnover is
smaller than highway mileage.

Through the elasticity analysis, we can understand the influencing mechanism of the factors. With the development of the Chinese economy in the "new
normal" period, China's transportation industry is expected to also change and
develop new characteristics under "new normal" development. Although the
demand for road transportation is currently increasing, this growth rate may
decline in future. As a result, the core influencing factors of road transport energy
consumption and the accurate prediction of road transport energy consumption
is of great significance for adapting the "new normal".

3.3.1 ETS and ARIMA models

The ETS model includes two different types. When assuming that $y_t = \mu_t + \varepsilon_t$,
the ETS model can be classified as an *additive errors model*. When assuming that
$y_t = \mu_t (1 + \varepsilon_t)$, the ETS model can be classified as a *multiplication errors model*.
The error, trend and seasonal components in the ETS model represent the error
term, trend term and season term, respectively, in which the trend and seasonal
groups include 15 models. The residual error term is classified as an overlapping

form (addition forms) and a multiplication form. When considering the different error forms, these 15 models can be extended to 30 types (Hyndman et al., 2008).

Because logarithmic data is steadier, it can eliminate heterovariance. In addition, logarithmic data is able to convert a nonlinear relationship between data (power function and exponential function relationships) into a linear relationship. Therefore, in this chapter, we will hereafter use logarithmic values for the two variables in our forecasting. The logarithmic values for road transport energy consumption use computational solutions (FORECAST Program Package of R) from the 30 ETS models and over a hundred ARIMA models, a selection from the information criterion – Akaike information criterion (AIC), Corrected Akaike's Information Criterion (AICc) and Bayesian Information Criterion (BIC) – and a forecast precision comparison. The parameter estimation results for the ETS and ARIMA models are shown in Table 3.13.

ETS (A,A,N) model for road transport energy consumption logarithm follows Equations 3.9 and 3.10.

$$y_t = l_{t-1} + b_{t-1} + \varepsilon_t, y_{t+1} = l_{t-1} + 2b_{t-1} + \varepsilon_t, \cdots,$$
$$y_{t+h-1} = l_{t-1} + hb_{t-1} + \varepsilon_t \qquad (3.9)$$

$$l_t = l_{t-1} + b_{t-1} + a\varepsilon_t, \ b_t = b_{t-1} + \beta a\varepsilon_t, \ \varepsilon_t \sim NID(0, \sigma^2),$$
$$0 < a < 1, \ 0 < \beta < a \qquad (3.10)$$

In these recursive equations, l_t indicates the intercept at time t; b_t indicates the slope at time t; S_t indicates the seasonal component at time t; m indicates the number of seasons (the cycle number is 12 and 4 in monthly data and quarterly data); α, β, r and φ are estimated constant values; h indicates the lag period; and $\varepsilon_t \sim NID(0, \sigma^2)$ is an error term.

Table 3.13 Univariate forecast model selection and precision analysis for logarithmic values

	Parameter	Logarithm values for ATTV	
	Model	*ETS(A,A,N)*	*ARIMA(0,1,0)*
Forecast precision	ME	0.001103443	0.0002044084
	RMSE	0.063297360	0.0632740300
	MAE	0.045906790	0.0458141600
	MPE	0.003087043	1.0783831000
	MAPE	0.457436200	−0.0059639520
	MASE	0.476953700	0.4564660000
Model selection	AIC	−66.06	−99.68
	AICc	−64.95	−99.35
	BIC	−59.20	−96.30

Notes: ETS(A,A,N) = Exponential Smoothing (Error, Trend, Seasonal); ARIMA(0,1,0) = Autoregressive Integrated Moving Average Model (p,d,q); ME = Mean Error; RMSE = Root Mean Squared Error; MAE = Mean Absolute Error; MPE = Mean Percentage Error; MAPE = Mean Absolute Percentage; MASE = Mean Absolute Scaled Error; AIC = Akaike's Information Criterion; AICc = corrected Akaike's Information Criterion; BIC = Bayesian Information Criterion

Forecasts from ETS(A,A,N)

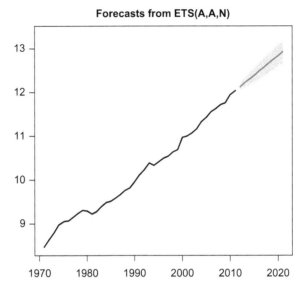

Forecasts from ARIMA(0,1,0) with drift

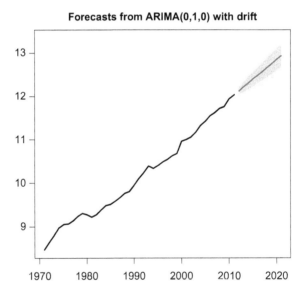

Figure 3.3 ETS forecast chart (L) and ARIMA forecast chart (R) for the logarithmic
values for road transport energy consumption

Figure 3.3 and Table 3.16 give the logarithmic forecast results for road transport energy consumption. The models were compared and screened using forecast precision methods. The predictive results of the ETS and the ARIMA were
very close. The ARIMA model is theoretically suitable for annual data forecasting. However, the ETS model is also available for such data forecasting because
of its nonstationary and nonlinear features. We can see from Table 3.16 that road

transport energy consumption index is nonstationary variable data, rather than periodic, which suggests that road transport energy consumption demand trend is more significant and that results predicted by the ETS model may be more accurate.

However, the univariate time series forecasts were obtained using the historical memorability rule from the time series analysis theory. In practical applications, the existence of uncertainty makes forecasting difficult, so in practice, we need to assume a future scenario analysis situation for the target variables. Therefore, we also used scenario analysis to forecast the road energy consumption demand. In Section 3.2, the driving factors and constraints were distinguished, but because there are multiple factors, we need to consider the overall effect of the market so as to avoid multicollinearity between the various factors. To solve this problem, we present the Bayesian model average method to select the model and filter the core factors.

3.3.2 Scenario analysis and synthesis

Bayesian model average

In 1978, the framework for the Bayesian model average (BMA) was proposed by Leamer (1978), who claimed that the model would be able to solve model uncertainty problems when choosing models. The basic idea of the BMA approach is that each model is neither fully accepted or nor entirely rejected. The prior probability of each model should be assumed first, and then a posterior probability is determined by extracting the data set that contains information and from the models' reception to dependent variables. The excellence of the BMA approach is not only that it can sort the influencing factors according to their importance, but that it can also calculate the posterior mean, standard deviation and other indicators for the corresponding coefficients. Based on this, this chapter uses the Markov chain Monte Carlo (MCMC) method for Bayesian model average calculation and confirms the weight distribution of the model according to prior information. (Green, 1995; Godsill, 2001). The MCMC method can overcome the shortcomings of the BIC, AIC and EM methods and has further advantages. First, when using different conditional probability distributions, the algorithms do not need to be changed. Second, the MCMC method seriously considers the weight and variance of the posterior distribution. Third, the MCMC simulation can deal with the high correlation parameters of the Bayesian model average.

Y is the predictive variable, $M = \{m_1, m_2, \ldots, m_k\}$ is the set of models under consideration, $p(m_k)$ is the prior probability that m_k is the true model, θ_k is the parameter for m_k, σ_k is the variance in m_k, $p(\theta k \mid mk)$ is the prior density of the parameters, $D = (y_1, y_2 \ldots y_T)^T$ is the given sample data, y_T is the observation data at T, and $p(D|m_k)$ is the marginal likelihood function. Thus, the posterior distribution for y given data D is calculated in Equation 3.11.

$$p\left(y \middle| m_1, m_2, \cdots m_k, D\right) = \sum_{k=1}^{K} p\left(y \middle| m_k, D\right) p\left(m_k \middle| D\right) \qquad (3.11)$$

Where $p(D|m_k)$ is the posterior probability. This indicates each prediction model's probability for describing the actual process. $p(y|m_k,D)$ is the posterior distribution of y when the model and data are given. The posterior distribution for y is given by Equation 3.12.

$$p\left(y\big|m_{1,}m_2,\cdots m_k,D\right) = \sum_{k=1}^{K} p\left(y\big|m_k,D\right)p\left(m_k\big|D\right) \tag{3.12}$$

This is an average of the posterior predictive distribution for y under each of the models considered, which is weighted by the corresponding posterior model probability. The posterior probability for model m_k is given by Equation 3.13.

$$p\left(m_k\big|D\right) = \frac{p\left(m_k\right)p\left(D\big|m_k\right)}{\displaystyle\sum_{j=1}^{K} p\left(m_j\right)p\left(D\big|m_j\right)} \tag{3.13}$$

Where, $p(D|m_k)$ is the integrated likelihood of model m_k, as shown in Equation 3.14.

$$p\left(D\big|m_k\right) = \int p\left(D\big|\theta_k,m_k\right)p\left(\theta_k\big|m_k\right)d\theta_k \tag{3.14}$$

Where $p(\theta_k|m_k)$ is the prior density of the parameters under model m_k, and $p(D|\theta_k,m_k)$ is the likelihood. All probabilities are implicitly conditional on M, the set of all models being considered.

Parameter estimates and other quantities of interest are provided by a straightforward application of the principles described earlier in this section. For example, the BMA estimate for a parameter θ_k is calculated by Equation 3.15.

$$\hat{\theta}_{BMA} = \sum_{k=1}^{K} \hat{\theta}_k p\left(M_k\big|D\right) \tag{3.15}$$

Where $\hat{\theta}_k$ denotes the posterior mean for model k. Variances in these estimates and other quantities are also available (Hoeting et al., 1999; Viallefont et al., 2001).

The predicted value for the minimum mean variance was calculated according to the mathematical expectations of Equation 3.13.

$$E_{BMA}\left(y\big|D\right) = \sum_{k=1}^{K} p\left(m_k\big|D\right)E\left[p_k\left(y\big|m_k,D\right)\right] = \sum_{k=1}^{K} w_k m_k \tag{3.16}$$

Equation 3.16 indicates the weighted average of all possible predictions $E(y|m_k,D)$ and is based on the posterior probability of the model $p(m_k|D)$ as the weight ($w_k = p(m_k|D)$).

The data include nine variables, which means $2^9 = 512$ model combinations. Let us focus on the unit information prior (UIP) g-prior (in this case, $g = N = 11$)

Table 3.14 The results of the BMA method

	PIP	Post Mean	Post SD	Cond.Pos.Sign
P	0.40985	7.41573250	10.97753831	1.0000000
Urban	0.30460	0.80139690	1.84856988	0.8945831
GDP	0.29028	0.15877940	0.31451397	0.9984153
CMT	0.22436	0.05910927	0.14911582	0.9999554
Credit	0.13151	−0.00516038	0.02821966	0.1275188

and assume uniform model priors. We calculated the posterior probability for the different models and selected the best five. The BMA results are shown in Table 3.14 (BMS Program Package of R). The second column (Post Mean) displays the coefficients averaged over all models. The coefficients' posterior standard deviations (Post SD) give further evidence. The importance of the variables in explaining the data is given in the first column (PIP), which shows the posterior inclusion probabilities. The sum of the PMPs is for all models in which a covariate is included. In fact, the coefficient sign can also be inferred from the fourth column (Cond.Pos.Sign), which is the posterior probability of a positive coefficient expected value conditional on the inclusion of "sign certainty". The importance of the influencing factors can be seen from the PIP index, in which it can be seen that population> urbanization rate > GDP > core business taxes and extra car manufacturing charges > automobile credit. The Cond.Pos.Sign size sorting results in population > core business tax and extra car manufacturing charges > GDP > urbanization rate > automobile credit.

The best five simple linear models sort the population, urbanization rate, GDP, core business taxes, extra car manufacturing charges and automobile credit as separate independent variables. However, the PIP value for core business taxes, extra car manufacturing charges and automobile credit are very small. As a result, the explanatory power of the two factors on road transport energy is small, and estimates for these two indicators are not available. Next, in the analysis of population size, multicollinearity was found between population and the urbanization rate. Therefore, we only consider the urbanization rate and GDP index as core factors for road transport energy consumption when establishing the multivariate regression model.

Multivariate regression model

The multivariate regression model is shown in Equation 3.17.

$$\ln y = 0.33 \ln GDP + 1.26 \ln urban + 2.66 \tag{3.17}$$

We are then able to give a scenario analysis for the core effect factors from 2012 to 2015. According to China's 12th Five-Year Plan, China's gross domestic product (GDP) in 2015 is estimated to be 55.8 trillion RMB, and the average annual growth, 7 per cent. Therefore, we calculated the annual average growth of GDP as 7 per cent. Urbanization is expected to be 54 per cent in 2015 as it

Table 3.15 Baseline scenario for core effect factors

Independent variable	GDP	Urbanization rate
2012	459336.20	52.2954
2013	491489.74	53.3413
2014	525894.01	54.4081
2015	562706.60	55.4963
2016	602096.06	56.6062
2017	644242.79	57.7384
2018	689339.78	58.8931
2019	737593.57	60.0710
2020	789225.10	61.2724
2021	844470.90	62.4978

had reached 51.27 per cent in 2011. After the 18th Communist Party of China (CPC) National Congress, the Chinese government has focused efforts on bridging the gap between the rich and the poor to ensure sustainable economic development. The most important measure to complete this goal is urbanization. To narrow the gap between the rich and poor, infrastructure, industrial transfers and structural adjustment in the process of urbanization are expected to lead to increased investment and employment. Therefore, urbanization is unlikely to decline in the future. Most population experts estimate that, after the 18th CPC National Congress, urbanization will reach more than 60 per cent by 2020. According to this forecast, urbanization annual growth is expected to reach about 2 per cent; so here, we assume a standard growth rate of 2 per cent for China's urbanization rate from 2011–2021, the results of which are shown in Table 3.15.

3.3.3 Combination forecast

Considering that the single variable time series recursive model and multiple regression model have different advantages and disadvantages (in prediction), we combined the results of the two models to conduct a combinational forecast. In 1969, Bates and Granger proposed combinational forecasting to cover all aspects of effective information, so as to avoid single forecast models under complex environments which could limit the predictions. The key to combinational forecast is to determine the weighting coefficients for every single forecast model. Kurz-Kim (2008) analyzed the weighting coefficients in a combinational forecast and selected the same weighting coefficient for every single forecast model because it was thought that, if different weighting coefficients were first selected, the combinational forecast would lose its meaning. It was therefore proven that the equally weighted combinational forecast had good rationality and applicability. The results of combinational forecast are shown in Table 3.16.

The univariate forecast value for the time series technology is larger than that of the multivariate regression under a scenario analysis. In other words, if historic development trends remain unchanged, road transport energy demand is expected to grow significantly. This is mainly because the multivariate regression forecast

Table 3.16 Forecasting results for road transport energy consumption

Model	ETS	ARIMA	Multivariate Bayesian regression model	Combination forecasting model
2012	185210.82	188401.39	154522	175994.1
2013	202169.15	209537.92	162003.1	191236.7
2014	220861.26	233048.07	169846.3	207918.6
2015	241281.60	259193.46	178069.3	226181.4
2016	263589.96	288272.07	186690.4	246184.1
2017	287960.90	320612.98	195728.8	268100.9
2018	314585.13	356582.18	205204.8	292124.1
2019	343674.41	396590.68	215139.7	318468.3
2020	375449.78	441083.73	225555.5	347363.0
2021	410163.03	490568.40	236475.5	379069.0
Annual growth rate	9.25%	11.2%	4.84%	8.9%

takes into account changing trends in the core effect factors in the decomposition index. With the development of the Chinese economy into a "new normal" period, the government believes that GDP and urbanization growth will enter a "new normal" and eventually slow down. However, many factors that have not been considered may have important effects in the future, such as those factors discussed in Section 3.2.3. Therefore, it is likely that such factors may eliminate the unfavorable influences caused by the core effect factors selected in this chapter. As a result, the predicted value for the multivariate regression model is smaller than for the univariate model. The univariate time series recursion model and the multivariate regression model have their own advantages and disadvantages.

3.4 Conclusions and policy implications

In 2014, the Chinese economy officially entered a "new normal" period. As the fundamental service industry for economic and social development, transportation should also actively adapt to this "new normal" period. In this chapter, we first analyzed the historical trends of total road turnover and GDP in the United States, Japan, the European Union and China. The two indexes presented an obviously "Inverted L" type pattern. At the same time, we explored the potential relationship between total road turnover, GDP and road transport energy consumption as total turnover and GDP were considered the main influencing factors on road transport energy consumption. Next, we employed a path analysis method to analyze the impact mechanism of the factors related to road transport energy consumption. Then, we adopted a BMA model to select the core factors related to road transport energy consumption in China. Finally, on the basis of model selection as well as a univariate (ETS and ARIMA models) and multivariate (multiple regression) analysis, road transport energy consumption was analyzed and forecast.

The elasticity analysis results showed that the order of elasticity for the different factors was urbanization rate > average number of automobile manufacturing employees > highway mileage > GDP > auto industry output > auto manufacturing: main business taxes and surcharges > total road turnover. Road transport energy consumption was found to rise by 0.58 per cent for every percentage point increase in GDP, by 0.34 per cent for total road turnover increase, by 0.9 per cent when highway mileage increased by 1 percentage point, by 2.83 when there was a 1 percentage point increase in urbanization, by 0.41 per cent when core business taxes and extra automobile manufacturing industry charges rose by one percentage point, by 0.54 per cent when there was a 1 percentage point in automobile industry output by value, and by 1.03 per cent when there was a 1 percentage point increase in the number of employees working in the automobile manufacturing industry. The urbanization rate was found to be the most elastic, followed by the average number of automobile manufacturing employees, both of which were found to be more than 1 per cent. The total turnover index was found to be not only a reflection of road transportation demand but also to include social and economic influences.

The forecast results demonstrated that road transport energy consumption would be expected to rise by 0.33 per cent with every 1 percentage point in GDP and road transport energy consumption would rise by 1.26 per cent for every 1 percentage point increase in the urbanization ratio. Road transport energy consumption in China reached about 379,069 kt of oil equivalent by 2021.

With the rapid development of the economy, industrialization and urbanization continue to accelerate, which increases the demand for transportation. To face the pressure of economic downturn, transportation infrastructure construction plays a key role in maintaining steady economic growth. However, the "new normal" of economic and social development requires that traffic energy consumption and pollution emissions be reduced and that the growth rate in road transport demand be slowed by changing traffic structures and improving fuel economies and traffic transportation efficiency. According to the analysis and forecast results, we offer the following suggestions.

Road transport energy consumption has increased annually, so transportation emissions reduction pressure is increasing. The challenge for the Chinese government is finding a way to realize the green development of transportation and developing new ways for green low-carbon cycle development in the "new normal" period. The government needs to prioritize busses to solve urban congestion problems and needs to encourage people to drive green. Transportation investment and financing reform are key areas and key links, and the government should strengthen automobile credit market regulation, improve the control of automobile credit funds, manage private car parking, collect congestion charges and plan low-emission zones to reduce private car purchases and travel times. The automobile manufacturing industry should optimize its industrial layout by taking innovation as its fundamental driving force, by implementing technical production and by enhancing the level of independent innovation and endogenous growth momentum. At the same time, it needs to develop new-energy vehicles and efficient low-energy products. With international development as a strategic target, it also needs to increase car exports. Therefore, the industry can achieve emissions reductions through technological progress as well as by controlling employment.

4 Aviation fuel demand development in China

This chapter analyzes the core factors and the impact path of aviation fuel demand in China and conducts a structural decomposition analysis of aviation fuel cost changes and the increase in the main aviation enterprises' business profits. Through the establishment of an integrated forecast model for China's aviation fuel demand, this chapter confirms that the significant rise in China's aviation fuel demand because of increasing air services demand is more than offset by higher aviation fuel efficiency. Few studies use a predictive method to decompose, estimate and analyze future aviation fuel demand. Based on a structural decomposition with indirect prediction, aviation fuel demand is decomposed into efficiency and total amount (aviation fuel efficiency and air transport total turnover). The core influencing factors for these two indexes are selected using path analysis. Then, univariate and multivariate models (ETS and ARIMA models and Bayesian multivariate regression) are used to analyze and predict both aviation fuel efficiency and air transport total turnover. Last, by integrating results, future aviation fuel demand is forecast. The results show that aviation fuel efficiency goes up by 0.8 per cent as the passenger load factor increases 1 per cent and the air transport total turnover goes up by 3.8 per cent and 0.4 per cent as the urbanization rate and the per capita GDP increase 1 per cent respectively. By the end of 2015, China's aviation fuel demand will have increased to 28 million tons, and is expected to be 50 million tons by 2020. With this in mind, increases in the main aviation enterprises' business profits must be achieved through the further promotion of air transport.

4.1 Introduction

The air transportation industry is rapidly developing in China and around the world. According to the Civil Aviation Administration of China (CAAC) (www.caac.gov.cn/index.html), by 2030, it is expected that 1.5 billion passengers annually will be travelling by air. The Promotion of Civil Aviation Industry Development report issued by the State Council (www.gov.cn/zhengce/content/2012-07/12/content_3228.htm) in 2012 estimated that the total aviation transport traffic in China would reach 170 billion km in 2020, a 12.2 per cent annual average growth. Because of the rapid growth in the aviation industry in China, the total aviation fuel consumption is also expected to increase significantly.

Air transport is a capital- and technology-intensive industry. Homogeneity of products and excessive competition have resulted in a less-than-average profit for the entire industry. Therefore, improving fuel efficiency and reducing running costs have become important to enhance the enterprises' competitive power. Annual reports for 2011 for Air China Limited, Hainan Airlines Company Limited, China Eastern Airlines Company Limited and China Southern Airlines Company Limited reported that the fuel costs for Air China were 33.79 billion RMB, an increase of 10.33 billion RMB with 44.01 per cent growth year-on-year and exceeded the net profit of 7.48 billion RMB in that year. In the same year, China Eastern Airlines' running costs were 70.45 billion RMB, of which fuel alone cost 29.23 billion RMB, resulting in a 9 per cent profit decline to 4.89 billion RMB. At present, the fuel costs of the three state-owned enterprises, Air China, China Eastern Airlines and China Southern Airlines, account for 40 per cent of overall operating costs.

Along with economic growth and the increase in air transport volume, the negative environmental impact of the aviation transportation industry is also being paid increasingly serious attention. The Intergovernmental Panel on Climate Change (IPCC) released "Aviation Activities and Global Climate" (Penner, 1999), which comprehensively analyzed the impact of aviation activities on the environment for the first time. This report pointed out that emissions were expected to continually increase with economic growth. At the same time, the EU aviation carbon tax is another challenge for aviation-caused environmental pollution. With rising oil prices and the increasing fixed costs for energy saving airplanes, an analysis of aviation fuel demand is important for improving fuel efficiency, for controlling aviation fuel costs and for reducing aviation industry carbon emissions.

Against this background, this chapter attempts to analyze and forecast aviation fuel demand trends by analyzing the current aviation fuel demand in China. This chapter has five parts. In this introduction, we will describe the realistic background for the research topic. In Section 4.2, we will present research on aviation fuel demand which introduces the academic background for the research topic. In Section 4.3, we will provide a structural decomposition analysis of aviation fuel consumption. We will analyze in detail the structural decomposition on aviation fuel efficiency, total air transport turnover and aviation fuel costs. In Section 4.4, we will also analyze and forecast aviation fuel demand, aviation transport total turnover and aviation fuel efficiency using a univariate and multivariate analysis. In the final section, we will provide some conclusions and recommendations.

4.2 Research on aviation fuel demand

Aviation traffic is expected to grow at an annual rate of about 5 per cent until 2026, and aviation fuel demand is expected to increase by 3 per cent per annum. Therefore, aviation fuel is expected to be in short supply by or before 2026 (Nygren et al., 2009). Using Organization for Economic Co-operation and Development (OECD) data for North America, Europe, the Pacific region and individual developing countries, Mazraati and Alyousif (2009) built an aviation fuel demand model. The results showed that aviation fuel demand rises by less than 1 per cent with a 1-percentage point rise in passenger transport turnover. The aviation industry consumed approximately 12.7 per cent of all oil in the transportation sector in 2005 and experienced a 2.32 per cent annual growth recently, from 1995 to 2004. Mazraati and Faquih (2008) built aviation fuel demand models for two different markets, among which the US was identified as a mature market and China as a rapidly developing market. Based on data such as aviation passenger transport turnover, freight transport turnover and the airline load factor in these two countries, in combination with economic growth and oil price fluctuations, a constant elasticity logarithmic model was developed. The findings demonstrated that aviation transport demand has greater price elasticity and is more sensitive to short-term economic waves in mature markets like the US compared to the rapidly developing aviation industry in China. The worldwide aviation industry accounts for 11.2 per cent of oil demand across the transportation industry, making it the second largest oil consumer. Aviation oil consumption accounts for 5.8 per cent of world oil consumption. The regional calculation economic model, built by Mazraati (2010), showed that aviation fuel demand lacked price elasticity, but there was a strong functional relationship between this demand and economic growth. While aviation fuel demand intensity across the world is continually reducing, it is expected that aviation fuel demand will increase to 2.7 million barrels per day (mb/d) by 2030, quite a significant proportion of which (0.75 mb/d) will come from China.

Using quarterly data from 1998 to 2009, Boshoff (2010) used an autoregression distribution lagging model and an ordinary particular method to estimate the price and income elasticity of aviation kerosene demand in South Africa. The results showed that aviation kerosene demand had low price elasticity but much higher income elasticity. Wadud et al. (2009) classified American citizens into five groups by income level and estimated the oil demand elasticity of these groups to examine the heterogeneity of oil demand changes at different income levels. The research found that the oil demand elasticity in different population groups was different, with the demand elasticity by income level from low to high showing a U-type pattern. Chèze et al. (2011) deployed a dynamic face-plate data calculation model to predetermine aviation fuel demand worldwide and across eight classified geographic regions and demonstrated that global aviation transport demand would increase by 100 per cent from 2008 to 2025 with an annual average growth rate of 4.7 per cent, while global aviation fuel demand was estimated to grow by 38 per cent with an annual average growth rate of 1.9 per cent. According to such findings, as aviation transport demand increases, improvements in aviation fuel efficiency could reduce aviation fuel demand. However, unless aviation technology changes or employs new energy sources, or unless aviation travel demand is restricted, there is little possibility that aviation fuel demand will decrease. Through an investigation focused on aviation fuel manufacturers and sellers in China, Zhao and Hu (2002) came to some important conclusions. Primarily, they found that aviation fuel production and delivery costs in China were much higher and concluded that, if resource distribution efficiencies are not improved, aviation fuel demand would continue to grow and would exceed supply in the first decade of the twenty-first century.

This research review indicates that aviation fuel demand has obvious driving factors. Economic development boosts aviation demand growth (Wells, 1988; Vedantham and Oppenheimer, 1998; Bernstein, 2002), which increases aviation fuel consumption. However, there are some factors which can lead to a reduction in aviation fuel consumption, such as pollution controls, intelligent aviation technology, improvements in three aviation activity efficiencies and engine fuel efficiency improvements (Babikian et al., 2002; Kick et al., 2012). Further, changes in aviation fuel prices (Adams and Gerner, 2012; Ryerson and Hansen, 2013) and fuel fee policies could also influence aviation fuel demand. Thus, when forecasting aviation fuel demand, changing trends in related areas need to be considered.

In sum, aviation fuel forecasting techniques can be classified as univariate and multivariate. Univariate forecasts primarily focus on time series forecast analysis, while multivariate forecasts focus on scenario analysis regression models and structure time series models. The factors that impact aviation fuel demand can be divided into two groups: first, the influence on aviation demand, namely aviation total turnover, and second, the influence on aviation fuel efficiency from such areas as aviation transport control technology, engine technology and advanced aircraft materials.

Research on China's aviation fuel demand and related issues has been sparse. This chapter delves into this question further. To forecast fuel demand, a univariate prediction method is used to improve prediction accuracy, and a multivariate prediction is used to emphasize the significance of the economic analysis. The purpose of this chapter, however, is to provide a decision-making reference, so the analysis needs to consider the advantages of the univariate and multivariate prediction methods. Given this, we first conduct a structural decomposition of aviation fuel demand based on the principle of decomposition and multiple predictions and then conduct a predictive analysis with each decomposition variable using univariate prediction technology. Multivariate prediction is used on the decomposition variables to gain insights into the formation of China's aviation fuel demand change path. By examining changes in the core influencing factors, an in-depth analysis of possible novel research ideas and structures is conducted and predictions for the object variable are determined.

4.3 Structural decomposition analysis on aviation fuel consumption and cost

After conducting a related effect factors analysis, Mazraati (2009) and Mazraati and Faquih (2008) built direct models for aviation fuel demand and obtained sound results. In this chapter, from a more detailed analysis and investigation of aviation fuel consumption, we will build a model using an indirect method.

According to Vedantham and Oppenheimer (1998), aviation fuel consumption (million tons) = total turnover of air transport (million tons km) × aviation fuel efficiency (kg/ton) × $10e(-1)$. This chapter uses a path analysis method to make an intensive study of the air transport total turnover and aviation fuel efficiency using annual data, data from the *China Statistical Yearbook*, the *Transport Statistical Yearbook*, the WIND Database and the CEIC Database, for multiple years.

In structural decomposition analysis, many variable selection methods, such as cointegration analysis, Granger causality tests, autocorrelation analysis or partial correlation analysis, cannot be used to comprehensively process the multiple influencing factors for crude oil price at the same time. Therefore, a path analysis model is introduced to extract the core factors to allow for the calculation and analysis of the direct and indirect relationships between the various variables. In addition, many dimensionality reduction methods, such as principal components analysis, can be applied to extract those representative variables which have a lower dimensionality and sufficient information. But in an economic sense, this recombination of all the selected variables does not reduce the dimensionality of the explanatory variables. So, path analysis models can not only eliminate the impact of multicollinearity but also select fewer core influencing factors from numerous variables. Therefore, path analysis is selected for our structural decomposition analysis. Path analysis is a continuation of simple correlation analysis. From the multiple regression, a correlation coefficient is resolved, and the direct effect of a variable on a dependent variable, the indirect effect of other variables on the dependent variable and the combined effect can be expressed through a direct path, an indirect path and the total path coefficients (Chai et al., 2009).

The multiple linear regression specification is shown in Equation 4.1.

$$y = \beta_0 + \beta_1 x_1 + \beta_2 x_2 + \cdots + \beta_k x_k \tag{4.1}$$

Where the independent variables are $x_1, x_2, \ldots, x_k$, and the dependent variable is y. Suppose σ_y is a sample standard deviation of y and σ_x is a sample standard deviation of x_i; then, the standardized multiple linear regression model is obtained from Equation 4.1. Let $\beta_i' = \beta_i \dfrac{\sigma_{x_i}}{\sigma_y}$, β_i' be the standardized coefficient. It can be seen that this standardized coefficient is correlated with not only the regression coefficients but also the volatility of the independent variables. If the volatility (standard deviation of the independent variables) is large, the independent variable becomes more important; otherwise, it is less important. However, when using the formula to solve standardized coefficients, whether there is interaction between the variables or the impact of the effects of other variables is not considered. However, using a path analysis method, this problem can be easily solved.

The decomposition equation for the simple correlation coefficients can be expressed as in Equation 4.2.

$$\begin{cases} p_{1y} + r_{12} p_{2y} + \cdots + r_{1k} p_{ky} = r_{1y} \\ r_{21} p_{1y} + p_{2y} + \cdots + r_{2k} p_{ky} = r_{2y} \\ \quad \cdots \\ r_{k1} p_{1y} + r_{k2} p_{2y} + \cdots + p_{ky} = r_{ky} \end{cases} \tag{4.2}$$

Where r_{ij} represents the simple correlation coefficients of x_i and x_j, r_{iy} represents the simple correlation coefficients for x_i and y. This is the basic path analysis model. p_{iy} is the direct path, the partial correlation coefficient of x_i and y after standardization, which represents the direct effect of x_i on y, and the direct determination coefficient $R_i^2 = p_{iy}^2$; $r_{ij} p_{jy}$ is the indirect path which represents the indirect effect of x_i on y through x_j, and the indirect determination coefficient is $R_{ij}^2 = 2 p_{iy} r_{ij} p_{jy}$; $R(i)^2 = R_i^2 + \sum_{i \neq j} R_{ij}^2$ represents the combined effect of x_i on y, which is named the decision coefficient. $\sum_{i \neq j} r_{ij} p_{jy}$ represents the total indirect effect of x_i on the independent variable through all the other variables. These equations are used to decompose the simple correlation coefficient for each independent variable and dependent variable into p_{iy} (direct path effect) and $\sum_{i \neq j} r_{ij} p_{jy}$ (total indirect path effect). Because of complex interactions between economic phenomena, it is impossible to take all factors into account when building the model. Therefore, it is important to further calculate the path effect coefficient for the omitted variables and errors on the dependent variable, that is the residual effect, p_{ay}. The computational formula is expressed in Equation 4.3.

$$p_{ay} = \sqrt{1 - \sum_{i=1}^{k} p_{iy} r_{iy}} \tag{4.3}$$

If this residual effect is small, the path analysis has grasped the main variables, but otherwise, the path analysis may be missing some main factors, so other factors are needed for the analysis.

Path analysis is not an ordinary standard multiple linear regression analysis. It is not used to predict and control, nor is it correlation analysis because the path coefficients are vectors; if x_i and y swap, $p_{iy} \neq p_{yi}$. Path coefficient values can be greater than 1 or less than -1 in real numbers. The purpose of path analysis is to decompose the correlation coefficient of the independent variable x_i and the dependent variable y into a direct effect, p_{iy}, and an indirect effect, $r_{iy} p_{jy}$. It tells us the following: first, p_{iy} indicates the intrinsic effect of x_i on y, without considering the influence of other variables; second, in the complex correlations between several variables $x_1, x_2, \ldots, x_k$ and y, r_{iy} are unable to describe the full relationship between x_i and y, as there are indirect effects; third, it is meaningful for decision-making to find the paths of an independent variable's influence on y from these complex multiple correlations.

4.3.1 Structural decomposition analysis on aviation fuel efficiency

From our literature review, the "three efficiencies", aviation fuel prices, engine technology, raw materials used in airplanes, aviation management, airplane crew planning and flight scheduling are all factors that influence aviation fuel efficiency (AFE).

Based on the data review, the daily aircraft utilization rate, passenger load factor, overall load factor, jet fuel prices, technological advancements (substituted with time), passenger transport turnover, freight transport turnover, the number of civil aviation airlines and the number of civil aviation airports were selected as the interpretable variables (*China Statistical Yearbooks* from 1979 to 2011). These variables include the following:

- Air transport total turnover (the sum of freight transport turnover and passenger transport turnover)
- Passenger transport turnover (the product of the number of passengers and the transport distance in passengers/km)
- Freight transport turnover (the product of the freight tonnage and the transport distance in tons/km)
- Aviation fuel efficiency (the maximum flying distance of an airplane per liter of fuel measured in kg/ton-km)
- The overall load factor (the ratio of the real load capacity with the maximum load capacity of an on-schedule airplane)
- Daily aircraft utilization rate (the number of flight hours per day)
- Passenger load factor (the ratio of the actual number of passengers with the number of available seats)
- The urbanization rate (the proportion of all the cities and towns residents relative to total population)
- The real per capita GDP (the ratio of the real GDP to total population)
- The number of civil aviation airports (the number of airports used for civil aircraft activities)
- The number of civil aviation routes (the number of air routes used for civil aircraft aviation activities rather than military activities, such as national defense, policing or customs)
- Aviation fuel price
- Airline passenger numbers

Screened and examined using path analysis, two variables were used in the final model: the overall load factor (unit, per cent) and a time variable representing technology. y is the dependent variable, which represents aviation fuel efficiency (logistic aviation fuel consumption, unit: kg/ton-km); $x_i (i = 1, 2)$ is the independent variable, which represents the logistic passenger load factor and the logistic time factor (expressing the non-neutral technological advancement trends), and ε is the random error term. Using the variables data from 1979 to 2011, the correlative coefficient matrix between the variables was first determined, and then using Equations 4.2 and 4.3, the path coefficients between the variables were calculated: $p_{1y} = -0.215$, $p_{2y} = 0.986$. Thus, the determination coefficient $R^2 = \sum_{i=1}^{2} p_{iy} r_{iy} = 0.954$, which expresses the explanation capacity of the independent variables to the dependent variable, was 95.4 per cent; that is to say, the path analysis adequately covers the primary effect factors. These analysis results are shown in Table 4.1.

The table shows that all variables pass the T-test and the path coefficient is evident. Table 4.1 shows that both the direct effect and combined effect of two variables

Table 4.1 Path analysis for the effect of the overall load factor and technological advancement on aviation fuel efficiency

	Combined effect against AFE	Direct effect against AFE	Indirect action	Decision coefficient	T-test
Overall load factor	−0.064	−0.215	0.151	−0.019	−5.328
Technological advancement (*t*)	−0.953	−0.986	0.033	0.907	−24.42

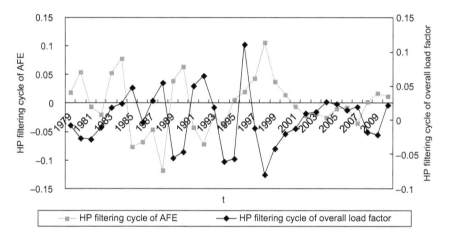

Figure 4.1 HP filter cycle fluctuation term for overall load factor and fuel efficiency

on aviation fuel efficiency are sequenced as (sequenced by absolute value) $x_1 < x_2$. The aviation fuel efficiency unit in this chapter is kg/ton-km, and when this figure is smaller, the efficiency is higher. Thus, both the overall load factor (unit: per cent) and the logistic time factor are able to boost aviation fuel efficiency. No matter whether it is a direct effect or a combined effect, the effect of technological advancement is quite obvious. In practical life, both the aviation overall load factor and the technological advancement factor boost aviation fuel efficiency, which can cut costs. Therefore, the direct effect of these two variables is greater than the combined effect (0.215 > 0.064; 0.986 > 0.953). At the same time, the variables' decision coefficient was calculated as: $R(1)^2 = -0.019$, $R(2)^2 = 0.907$. Thus, technological advancement can be seen to be a decisive factor impacting oil consumption, while the overall load factor is the main restraining factor.

Though this chapter quotes annual data, the attenuation characteristics of aviation fuel efficiency autocorrelation and partial correlation coefficients show stronger periodic behaviors. A Hodrick-Prescott (HP) filter decomposition of all variables found that the periodic characteristics of the overall load factor was closely linked with fuel efficiency and can be interpreted as the aviation fuel efficiency cycle and fluctuation (as shown in Figure 4.1). In addition, a simple correlation analysis proved the strong linear correlation (HP filter cycle term's correlation coefficient for aviation fuel efficiency and overall load factor was −0.715), which indicated that the fluctuation of load factor significantly influences the short-term fluctuations of aviation fuel efficiency, and an increase of the overall load factor can improve aviation fuel efficiency for a short time. The trend analysis showed that long-term aviation fuel efficiency trends are closely correlated with technological advancement. The HP filter trend term's correlation coefficient for aviation fuel efficiency and technological advancement was −0.98, which indicates that long-term and effective improvements in aviation fuel efficiency can be gained through continuing technological advancement.

4.3.2 Structural decomposition analysis on air transport total turnover

In line with this, a path analysis was conducted for the air transport total turnover (ATTT). From the analysis results, as the sum of freight transport and passenger transport turnover, the total aviation turnover is determined by such variables as economic development, consumption capability per capita, population structure, geographic location and the layout of other means of transport. Aviation transport supply is limited by the number of airlines, airports and airplanes. When demand exceeds supply, which sometimes happens in China, the supply actually determines the air transport total turnover. Therefore, here we choose the economy, population, income and related aviation transport supply indexes as the variables to interpret the air transport total turnover (megaton km).

Screened and examined using the path analysis, the following two variables were used in the final model: the urbanization rate (per cent) and real China's per capita GDP (RMB). y is an dependent variable, which represents the air transport total turnover (logistic total turnover); x_i ($i = 1, 2$) is an independent variable, which represents the logistic urbanization rate and the logistic real per capita GDP in China, and ε is the random error term. Using data from 1979 to 2011 for variables, the correlative coefficient matrix between the variables was first obtained, then using Equations 4.2 and 4.3, and the path coefficients between the variables were calculated as:

$p_{1y} = 0.623, p_{2y} = 0.391$. Thus, the determination coefficient $R^2 = \sum_{i=1}^{2} p_{iy} r_{iy} = 0.994$,

which expresses the explanation capacity of the independent variables to the dependent variable was 99.4 per cent, indicating that the path analysis adequately covers the primary effect factors. These analysis results are shown in Table 4.2.

Table 4.2 Path analysis for the effect of the proportion of urban residents and real GDP per capita on aeronautical transport total turnover

	Combined action against ATTT	Direct action against ATTT	Indirect action	Decision coefficient	T-test
Proportion of urban residents	0.986	0.623	0.363	0.840	14.425
Real GDP per capita	0.969	0.391	0.578	0.605	9.062

Table 4.2 shows that both the direct effect and combined effect of various variables against the air transport total turnover are sequenced (by absolute value) as $x_2 < x_1$. In other words, both the combined effect and the direct effect of urbanization significantly increase the air transport total turnover. Urbanization is one of the most important indicators for the closing of the per capita income gap in China and results in larger populations around airports, which can directly promote air transport demand. This conclusion has been reported by many previous studies.

4.3.3 Structural decomposition analysis on aviation fuel cost

In China, aviation enterprise airplanes are mostly acquired through operating or finance leases, so the cost of owning is generally higher than the international large airlines companies. Moreover, products and services, such as airborne equipment, maintenance, aircraft equipment and consumable parts, special vehicles, computer systems and other equipment, are purchased from foreign countries. So the cost of owning and operating airplanes is considered a fixed cost that does not change with usage, and which makes up a large proportion of the total costs. More than that, for policy reasons, China's aviation fuel price is much higher than the international average price.

The key to reducing total costs is to reduce the costs related to airplane ownership and operations as well as the costs related to aviation fuel consumption. In terms of fuel savings, in addition to air route distribution adjustments and flight skills improvements, the use of more fuel-efficient airplanes has become the first choice. However, at present, there are technological limits which increase the ownership and operating costs of these fuel-efficient airplanes.

In recent years, aviation enterprises have worked to control costs to differing degrees of success. However, as controllable costs make up only a small proportion of the total costs, cost control has not been very effective at reining in overall costs. In addition, during the same period, the uncontrollable costs have risen rapidly, offsetting any enterprise cost control effects. While aviation fuel consumption in China has been constantly increasing, world oil prices have also been increasing, which means that aviation fuel costs have become the highest cost item.

Suppose that Y is the costs of aviation fuel (1,000 dollars), A is air transport total turnover (million tons/km), B is aviation fuel efficiency (kg/ton-km), and C is the aviation fuel price (dollar/ton).

Therefore, $Y = A^*B^*C$, so we will use Equation 4.4.

$$\begin{aligned}
\Delta Y_t = Y_t - Y_0 &= A_t B_t C_t - A_0 B_0 C_0 \\
&= A_t B_t C_t - A_0 B_t C_t + A_0 B_t C_t - A_0 B_0 C_t \\
&\quad + A_0 B_0 C_t - A_0 B_0 C_0 \\
&= \Delta A_t B_t C_t + A_0 \Delta B_t C_t + A_0 B_0 \Delta C_t
\end{aligned}$$

(4.4)

Similarly, exchanging the order of the products for = A, B, C, the other five kinds of decomposition can be determined. To eliminate the middle items, these six kinds of decomposition are totaled and averaged, using Equation 4.5.

$$\Delta Y_t = Y_t - Y_0 = \Delta A_t (2B_t C_t + 2B_0 C_0 + B_0 C_t + B_t C_0) / 6$$
$$+ \Delta B_t (2A_t C_t + 2A_0 C_0 + A_0 C_t + A_t C_0) / 6 \qquad (4.5)$$
$$+ \Delta C_t (2A_t B_t + 2A_0 B_0 + A_0 B_t + A_t B_0) / 6$$

This equation shows that aviation fuel cost changes result from changes in efficiency, total turnover and price. This data for air transport total turnover (million tons/km) and aviation fuel efficiency (kg/ton-km) come from the 1996–2010 *China Statistical Yearbooks*, while the aviation fuel price (dollar/ton) was taken from the annual American aviation fuel spot price. In China, the aviation fuel spot price is set based on the aviation fuel price in Singapore and other places in accordance with certain National Development and Reform Commission (NDRC) criteria. Generally, as the air industry is a global industry, there is little difference between aviation fuel price trends, amplitude, or direction around the world, which means that the annual aviation fuel price correlation in different markets is close to 1. That is to say, in this chapter, aviation fuel prices in both China and the US have a very significant linear relationship which has a constant coefficient ratio. Therefore, in the calculation process, the constant coefficient can be eliminated, which has little effect on the final results. The specific calculations are as in Table 4.3.

An improvement in aviation fuel efficiency can be seen to reduce aviation fuel costs. The data in Table 4.3 also shows that aviation fuel efficiency has a negative contribution most of the time. In 1997, each ton/km aviation fuel consumption rose from 0.43 kg/ton-km in 1996 to 0.44 kg/ton-km, so aviation fuel efficiency

Table 4.3 Structural decomposition analysis for aviation fuel cost changes

Year	Cost changes for aviation fuel (1,000 dollars)	Contribution ratio for aviation fuel efficiency changes	Contribution ratio for air transport total turnover changes	Contribution ratio for aviation fuel price changes	Total
1996	158390	0	39.286	60.714	100
1997	21573	64.917	204.959	−169.876	100
1998	−107266	−23.594	−37.236	160.830	100
1999	129038	−40.766	58.989	81.777	100
2000	526097	−8.352	24.355	83.997	100
2001	−62568	88.657	−258.922	270.265	100
2002	42234.06	−122.017	415.098	−193.081	100
2003	250132	−14.174	17.770	96.404	100
2004	1122459	−6.462	51.295	55.166	100
2005	1516851	−3.175	26.326	76.849	100
2006	1258328	−10.050	58.005	52.045	100
2007	1181669	−28.229	88.298	39.932	100
2008	3031434	2.541	8.121	89.338	100
2009	−3567791	2.823	−27.565	124.742	100
2010	3419453	−7.341	51.032	56.309	100

dropped, which can be seen to have had a positive contribution to rising costs. In 1998, the efficiency decreased further as ton/km fuel consumption rose from 0.44 kg/ton-km in 1997 to 0.46 kg/ton-km in 1998. However, over this period, costs dropped to $107,266. So, here we can see that the larger (lower) efficiency value saw lower costs, meaning that fuel efficiency had a negative contribution to costs. In 2001, efficiency improved, in which the ton/km fuel consumption fell from 0.4 kg/ton-km in 2000 to 0.38 kg/ton-km in 2001. In 2001, costs also dropped, so, the improved efficiency had a positive contribution on costs. In 2008, the situation was the same as in 1997, 2001 and 2009.

An increase of the air transport total turnover can be seen to drive aviation fuel consumption and costs. From Table 4.3, we can see that total turnover is related positively to fuel costs increases most of the time. In 1998, the aviation transport total turnover rose, and costs were reduced, so, in this case, the total turnover played a negative role in the rising costs. From Table 4.3, we can see that total turnover has risen in all years. However, when total turnover does have a negative contribution to aviation fuel cost changes, costs are decreasing.

A rise in aviation fuel prices can be seen to drive aviation fuel costs. However, in 1997, 1998, 2001, 2002 and 2009, there was a decline in aviation fuel prices. Accordingly, in 1998, 2001 and 2009, there was a decline in aviation fuel costs, so this reduced price had a positive contribution to reduced costs in these three years. In 1997 and 2002, there was a rise in aviation fuel costs, so the reduced price had a negative contribution to the rise in these two years.

In general, aviation fuel costs declined in the three years from 1997 to 2010, namely 1998, 2001 and 2009. The primary causes were the reduced price of aviation fuel in 1998, and enhanced efficiency and reduced aviation fuel prices in 2001 and 2009.

The main aviation enterprise business profit equals the main business income the main business costs minus business tax and surcharges. Further, the final aviation enterprise profit is calculated from the main business profit, other operating profit, financial expenses, administration expenses, taxes and other activities. Many of these items are uncontrollable, but both main business income and main business costs can be controlled. Maximizing the difference between income and costs is therefore the best method to maximize profit.

From this analysis, it can be seen that the main business income (y_2) is a function of air transport total turnover (x_1), the market price index (p_1), with the consumer price index (CPI) instead) and the aviation fuel price (p_2). The main business costs (y_1) are a function of air transport total turnover (x_1), aviation fuel efficiency (x_2), aviation fuel price (p_2) and technological advancement (t). Suppose variable y denotes the difference between the main business income and the main business cost, as shown in Equation 4.6.

$$y_1 = f(x_1, x_2, t, p_2), \ y_2 = f(x_1, p_1, p_2), \ y = y_2 - y_1 = f(x_1, x_2, p_1, p_2, t) \ (4.6)$$

According to the construction principles for the production function and the cost function, we assume that there is a nonlinear relationship between the

Table 4.4 MCMC assessment results for the profit function

Node	Mean	Sd	MC error	2.5 per cent	Median	97.5 per cent	Start	Sample
c1	8.238	0.233	0.004	7.782	8.241	8.690	5000	5001
c2	−5.883	0.438	0.006	−6.753	−5.882	−5.010	5000	5001
c3	−1.191	0.242	0.004	−1.653	−1.198	−0.700	5000	5001
c4	−4.384	0.396	0.006	−5.147	−4.387	−3.612	5000	5001
c5	−0.473	0.022	0.000	−0.515	−0.473	−0.432	5000	5001
k	−22.370	0.437	0.007	−23.250	−22.370	−21.520	5000	5001

independent variables and variable y, which after the application of logarithmics becomes a linear relationship.

The profit function is built as shown in Equation 4.7.

$$\ln y = k_3 + c_1 \ln x_1 + c_2 \ln x_2 + c_3 \ln p_1 + c_4 \ln p_2 + c_5 \ln t \qquad (4.7)$$

Because of the small sample, we use MCMC arithmetic. Each iteration is performed 10,000 times. The first 5,000 iterations act as a drill sample, and the next 5,000 iterations act as an assessment sample, the results of which are shown in Table 4.4.

Table 4.4 shows that rising market price index and aviation fuel price lead to a rise in costs and a decline in aviation enterprise profits. Further, it can be seen that cost reductions due to technological innovation are unable to offset the costs of owning and operating the airplanes. Therefore, in China, under the current circumstances, increasing the main business profits depends on increasing total turnover.

4.4 Aviation fuel demand forecasting

Chatfield (1988) reviewed and divided forecasting methods into univariate, multivariate and judgment-based methods, or automatic and nonautomatic methods. "Optimum" method selection is decided by the various circumstances or effect factors which need to be considered. De Gooijer and Hyndman (2006) reviewed time series forecast research conducted over the past 25 years. During this period, over one-third of papers issued by core journals, the *Journal of Forecasting* from 1982–1985 and the *International Journal of Forecasting* from 1985–2005, were about time series forecasts with great progress being shown in some fields.

Forecast techniques can be classified as univariate (Fildes, 1983; Boutahar, 2007; Baghestani, 2010) and multivariate (Chigira and Yamamoto, 2009; Fukuda, 2009). Univariate mainly refers to time series forecasts and intelligent forecasts. Time series forecasts mostly utilize a smoothness forecasting model (Taylor, 2004; Gelper et al., 2010; Koehler et al., 2012) and the ARIMA forecasting model (Cholette, 1982; Bianchi et al., 1998; Butler, 1999). One important type of forecasting is combination forecasting (Chatfield, 1996; Guerrero and Peña, 2000; Meade, 2000; Kurz-Kim, 2008; Andrawis et al., 2011), which combines various information sources through the use of optimization.

In China, airplanes are mostly acquired on operating leases or financing leases. Products and services are most often purchased from foreign countries. Therefore, aviation fuel efficiency in China is about the same as it is internationally. However, aviation fuel consumption demand has had marked stage characteristics as the economy has developed.

This chapter selects five representative developed countries: France, Germany, Britain, Japan and the United States. Using data from the World Bank, we collected data from the economic indexes of these five countries, such as per capita GDP data from 1961 to 2012, freight transport turnover (million tons/km) and airline passenger numbers (person) from 1970 to 2012. Using an F-test, a T-test and simulation analysis for this time series data, the future development trends for aviation transport demand in China were estimated. The trend fitting functions based on the historical data from the five countries was calculated, the results of which are shown in Table 4.5, which shows the data for freight transport turnover and airline passenger numbers with the obvious nonlinear and nonstationary characteristics.

We also compared the annual value for the per capita freight transport turnover and the per capita passenger transport turnover in the five developed countries with the maximum values in China from 1970 to 2012. The specific results are shown in Figures 4.2 and 4.3.

In Figures 4.2 and 4.3, the per capita freight transport turnover = the actual cargo weight × the load distance/total population, the per capita airline passenger

Table 4.5 The trend fitting functions for the freight transport turnover and the airline passenger numbers in five developed countries

	Airline passenger number	R^2	Freight transport turnover	R^2	Property
Germany	$y = 5E + 0.6e^{0.073x}$	0.982	$y = -0.319x^3 + 21.34x^2 - 163.5x + 1037$	0.979	nonlinear
UK	$y = 1E + 0.7e^{0.051x}$	0.982	$y = 0.017x^4 - 1.764x^3 + 57.09x^2 - 454.6x + 1515$	0.911	nonlinear
France	$y = -622.7x^3 + 43208x^2 + 502 + 9E + 0.6$	0.981	$y = 293.2x^{0.816}$	0.964	nonlinear
Japan	$y = -3667x^3 + 19254x^2 + 171 + 2E + 0.7$	0.972	$y = 184.3x^{1.049}$	0.947	nonlinear
US	$y = -55756x^2 + 2E + 0.7x + 1E$	0.977	$y = 4988e^{0.052x}$	0.976	nonlinear

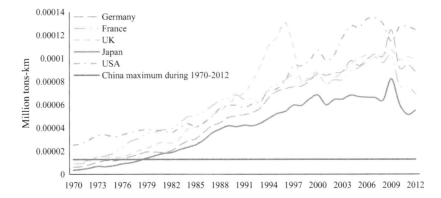

Figure 4.2 Comparison of the per capita freight transport turnover between China and developed countries

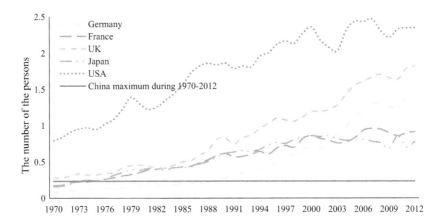

Figure 4.3 Comparison of the per capita passenger transport turnover between China and developed countries

number = the actual passenger number / total population. The per capita freight transport turnover in China reached a maximum of 1,285,330 tons/km per person in 2010; the per capita airline passenger numbers in China reached a maximum of 0.236 in 2012. These two maximum values are equal to those in France, Germany, Britain and Japan in the 1970s and 1980s and to that of the United States in the 1950s and 1960s. The developmental levels of per capita freight transport turnover and per capita airline passenger numbers in China have been far behind the developed countries for nearly 40 years. Therefore, according to the development trends in the aviation industry in the five developed countries, demand for air transport in China has significant room for growth in the future, with a parallel growth and increase in demand for aviation fuel.

According to this analysis and to De Gooijer and Hyndman (2006), air transport total turnover and aviation fuel efficiency are nonstationary data, with some levels of nonlinearity and periodicity. The prediction interval here is up to 2020. The original data sequences for the two variables have low volatility, but even for those with a higher volatility, as long as the predicted results appropriately reflect the variables' developmental trends, this kind of model can assure a proper forecast. Further, trend prediction in the ARIMA and ETS models has a significant advantage. It is generally believed that the ARIMA model is more general than the exponential smoothing model and has been widely used in practical applications. However, these two models mutually overlap; for example the linear exponential smoothing model is special to the ARIMA model. Hyndman et al. (2008) presented a discussion of these two models' equivalence. However, a nonlinear exponential smoothing model has no homologous equivalence to the ARIMA model. On the other hand, many ARIMA models do not have homologous equivalence with the exponential smoothing model. Thus, these two models partially overlap and have their own advantages and disadvantages. According to Hyndman et al. (2002), the ETS model is superior to the ARIMA for forecasting seasonal data, but for annual data forecasting, the ARIMA model is better because the selection of more ARIMA models may bring more uncertainties, resulting in poorer forecasting. However, pocket-sized ETS models are able to completely capture the uncertainties and dynamic features of the real economic or commerce time series data.

Based on this review, in this chapter, we will use a univariate ETS model and an ARIMA forecast model, both of which have been successfully used in the past but need further improvement, to analyze and forecast aviation fuel demand, in combination with a multivariate model.

4.4.1 ETS and ARIMA model and synthesis

As mentioned, in this chapter, we have chosen ETS (Exponential Smoothing Technology) and ARIMA (Autoregressive Integrated Moving Average) models to conduct the univariate forecasts for air transport total turnover and aviation fuel efficiency.

ETS technology appeared in and was widely used in the 1950s. After decades of development, it has matured significantly. However, the selection of an "optimum" model from the different models available began a few years ago. Hyndman et al. (2008) summed up exponential smoothing models and divided them into 15 types.

The error, trend and seasonal components in the ETS model represent the error term, trend term and season term, respectively, in which the trend and seasonal groups include 15 models. The residual error term is classified as an overlapping form (addition forms) and a multiplication form. When assuming $y_t = \mu_t + \varepsilon_t$, the ETS model can be classified as an *additive errors model*. When assuming $y_t = \mu_t (1 + \varepsilon_t)$, the ETS model can be classified as a *multiplication errors model*. When considering the different error forms, these 15 models can be extended to

30 types. From the forecast results alone, the addition form or the multiplication form do not greatly influence the residual error term. However, for differently sampled data, these various residual error forms are either superior or inferior. Because dividing by 0 is involved, attention needs to be paid to the selection of different addition or multiplication forms for the residual error, trend terms or season terms. When samples all have positive values, using the residual error multiplication form has advantages. However, when samples are zero or have a negative value, the multiplication form model is not applicable.

Because logarithmic data is steadier, it can eliminate heterovariance. In addition, logarithmic data is able to convert a nonlinear relationship (power function and exponential function relationships) between data into a linear relationship. Therefore, in this chapter, we hereafter use logarithmic values for the two variables in our forecasting. The logarithmic values for air transport total turnover and aviation fuel efficiency using the computational solutions (FORECAST program package of R) from the 30 ETS models and over a hundred ARIMA models, as well as through the selection of the information criterion (AIC, BIC, AICc) and a comparison of forecast precision, the model selection and precision statistics for the air transport total turnover and aviation fuel efficiency logarithmic values are shown in Table 4.6. The parameter estimation results for the ETS and ARIMA models are shown in Tables 4.7 and 4.8.

The exponential smoothing estimation models for aviation fuel efficiency and air transport total turnover logarithmic values were derived using Equations 4.8 and 4.9.

a) ETS (A,A$_d$,N) model for aviation fuel efficiency logarithm

$$y_t = l_{t-1} + \phi b_{t-1} + \varepsilon_t, y_{t+1} = l_{t-1} + (\phi + \phi^2)b_{t-1} + \varepsilon_t, \cdots, y_{t+h-1}$$
$$= l_{t-1} + (\phi + \phi^2 + \cdots + \phi^h)b_{t-1} + \varepsilon_t \qquad (4.8)$$

$$l_t = l_{t-1} + \phi b_{t-1} + a\varepsilon_t, \ b_t = \phi b_{t-1} + \beta a \varepsilon_t, \ \varepsilon_t \sim NID(0,\sigma^2),$$
$$0 < a < 1, \ 0 < \beta < a, \ 0 < \phi < 1$$

b) ETS (A,A,N) model for air transport total turnover logarithm

$$y_t = l_{t-1} + b_{t-1} + \varepsilon_t, y_{t+1} = l_{t-1} + 2b_{t-1} + \varepsilon_t, \cdots, y_{t+h-1} = l_{t-1} +$$
$$hb_{t-1} + \varepsilon_t \qquad (4.9)$$

$$l_t = l_{t-1} + b_{t-1} + a\varepsilon_t, \ b_t = b_{t-1} + \beta a \varepsilon_t, \ \varepsilon_t \sim NID(0,\sigma^2), 0 < a < 1, 0 < \beta < a$$

In these recursive equations, l_t indicates the intercept at time t; b_t indicates the slope at time t; S_t indicates the seasonal component at time t; m indicates the number of seasons (the cycle number is 12 and 4 in monthly data and quarterly data); α, β, r and φ are estimated constant values; h indicates the lag period; and $\varepsilon_t \sim NID(0, \sigma^2)$ is an error term.

Table 4.6 shows that the ARIMA model is superior to the ETS model in terms of forecasting precision. That the various data were nonstationary and

Table 4.6 Univariate forecast model selection and precision analysis for logarithm values for air transport total turnover (ATTT) and aviation fuel efficiency (AFE)

	Parameter	Logarithm values for ATTT		Logarithm values for AFE	
	Model	ETS(A,A,N)	ARIMA(0,1,0) with drift	ETS(A,Ad,N)	ARIMA(0,1,0) with drift
Forecast	ME	0.005	0.000	−0.001	0.000
precision	RMSE	0.084	0.083	0.057	0.060
	MAE	0.060	0.058	0.045	0.040
	MPE	0.052	0.004	−0.381	0.359
	MAPE	0.670	0.653	6.753	5.935
	MASE	0.395	0.386	0.886	0.794
Model	AIC	−36.748	−50.400	−62.245	−81.990
selection	AICc	−34.929	−49.880	−59.937	−81.560
	BIC	−31.564	−47.880	−54.916	−79.120

Table 4.7 Parameter estimation for ETS model for logarithmic values for air transport total turnover (ATTT) and aviation fuel efficiency (AFE)

Parameter estimation		Logarithm values of ATTT ETS(A,A,N)	Logarithm values of AFE ETS(A,A_d,N)
Smoothing parameters	c	0.758	0.703
	β	0.000	0.000
	ϕ		0.944
Initial states	l_0	7.164	−0.135
	b_0	0.137	−0.073
	σ	0.084	0.0572

Table 4.8 Parameter estimation for ARIMA model for logarithmic values for air transport total turnover (ATTT) and aviation fuel efficiency (AFE)

Parameter estimation	Logarithm values of ATTT ARIMA(0,1,0) with drift	Logarithm values of AFE ARIMA(0,1,0) with drift
Drift	0.142	−0.032
S.e.	0.017	0.011
σ^2	0.007	0.004
Log likelihood	27.200	43.000

cyclical when the variable analysis was conducted is shown in Section 4.3. The ARIMA model is theoretically suitable for annual data forecasting. However, the ETS model is also available for such data forecasting because of its nonstationary and nonlinear features. Further, the ETS estimation results are closer to the data in the 12th Five-Year Plan for the civil aviation industry, which stated that the trend characteristics were more evident for those target variables with certain cyclicity.

The set objective for air transport total turnover in the 11th Five-Year civil aviation industry plan was 50 billion tons/km, but the actual volume was 53.8 billion tons/km in 2010. For such a flourishing industry with tremendous development potential, it is reasonable that actual demand or consumption data was higher than the previously forecast or planned values. After restoring the logarithmic results in Table 4.9, the ETS forecast for air transport total turnover in 2015 was 101.12 billion tons/km, and the ARIMA forecast was 101.85 billion tons/km, while the scheduled value in the 12th Five-Year civil aviation industry program was 99 billion tons/km, which indicates that our forecast results are reasonable and effective.

The set objective for aviation fuel efficiency in the 11th Five-Year civil aviation industry program was 0.302 kg/ton-km fuel consumption, but the actual efficiency was 0.298 kg/ton-km in 2010. Factors such as advanced aviation engine technology, the deployment of new aviation materials, fleet renewal, intelligent aviation transport programming and modern air traffic control techniques have greatly boosted aviation fuel efficiency. It is difficult to accurately estimate the technical innovation and popularization speed in this field. Thus, it is reasonable to assume that actual growth generally exceeds planned growth. After restoring the logarithmic results, in Table 4.9, the ETS forecast for aviation fuel efficiency in 2015 was 0.285 kg/ton-km and the ARIMA forecast was 0.254 kg/ton-km, while the scheduled value in the 12th Five-Year civil aviation industry program was less than 0.294 kg/ton-km, which indicates that our forecast results are reasonable and effective. However, the ETS forecast was more reliable because improvements in fuel efficiency are expected to be increasingly difficult.

Restoring the forecast results for the two models, the forecasts for aviation fuel efficiency, air transport total turnover and fuel consumption demand are shown in Table 4.9.

Table 4.9 Forecasting result for the ETS and ARIMA models for aviation fuel demand

Model	ETS			ARIMA		
Parameter	AFE	ATTT	AFD	AFE	ATTT	AFD
Forecasting 2012	0.293	66988.750	1963.704	0.279	66545.420	1859.095
result 2013	0.290	76843.790	2229.362	0.271	76687.190	2074.387
2014	0.287	88149.540	2532.451	0.262	88375.490	2314.632
2015	0.285	101117.700	2878.288	0.254	101845.300	2582.703
2016	0.282	115993.600	3273.045	0.246	117366.900	2881.793
2017	0.280	133059.300	3723.792	0.238	135255.400	3215.551
2018	0.278	152634.300	4238.526	0.230	155870.400	3587.963
2019	0.276	175089.100	4826.505	0.223	179627.400	4003.503
2020	0.274	200849.300	5498.359	0.216	207003.300	4467.128

Note: Aviation fuel demand (AFD, per 10,000 tons); aviation fuel efficiency (AFE, per kg/ton-km); and air transport total turnover (ATTT, per megaton km)

4.4.2 Multivariate Bayesian regression model forecast and combination forecast

The univariate time series forecast results for aviation fuel demand resolved index and the combined forecast results for aviation fuel demand have been reported in earlier parts of this chapter. These forecasts were obtained through the historical memorability rule in time series analysis theory. In practical applications, the existence of uncertainty makes forecasting difficult. Hence, based on the assumption of uncertainty, a target variable forecast has been the basis for research organizations and government agencies to develop policies.

Here, we use circumstance analysis to forecast aviation fuel demand. On the basis of the variable analysis in Section 4.3, the core effect factors for aviation fuel efficiency and aviation total turnover were obtained. If a multivariate technique is used to forecast aviation fuel efficiency and aviation total turnover, the expected future value of these core effect factors must be available. Extant literature has mostly used scenario analysis to give the independent variable forecast values under high/low and high/medium/low uncertainties, and then these forecast values are substituted into the model to obtain the forecast values of the dependent variable. In different circumstances, the independent variable baseline scenario is the most important. Through a reasonable floatation, a good or poor circumstance analysis is given.

Along with information technological development, knowledge and technologies change regularly, which causes difficulties when seeking to forecast technological trends. While the development of knowledge and information is often a gradual and accumulative process, technical innovation often results in an abrupt change. The floatation of forecast values under a baseline scenario, therefore, cannot accurately reflect future changes in the pre-estimated variables. Therefore, here, we only give the baseline scenario and do not conduct pre-estimation under various circumstances. The future baseline scenario pre-estimated value for the core index related to aviation fuel efficiency is shown in Table 4.10.

Table 4.10 Baseline scenario for core effect factors for aviation fuel efficiency (AFE) and air transport total turnover (ATTT)

	Dependent variable	AFE		ATTT	
	Independent variable	Overall load factor (%)	Technological advancement trend	Urbanization rate (%)	Real GDP per capita (RMB)
Independent variable forecasting result	2012	0.723	3.555	52.295	2351.480
	2013	0.727	3.584	53.341	2516.083
	2014	0.730	3.611	54.408	2692.209
	2015	0.734	3.638	55.496	2880.664
	2016	0.738	3.664	56.606	3082.310
	2017	0.741	3.689	57.738	3298.072
	2018	0.745	3.714	58.893	3528.937
	2019	0.749	3.738	60.071	3775.963
	2020	0.753	3.761	61.272	4040.280

For aviation fuel efficiency, it can be seen that the overall load factor reached 71.6 per cent in 2010, while this rate in the 12th Five-Year civil aviation industry program is expected to be over 70 per cent in 2015. That is to say, this rate is expected to only slightly fluctuate in the future. In particular, the current overall load factor in China has been higher than the global average, and there is little space for further increases. So in 2011, the overall load factor only reached 72 per cent. Traffic infrastructure construction in China has been rapidly advancing but generally has been always behind economic development, and the aviation industry is no exception. According to the 12th Five-Year aviation industry program, there are expected to be 230 domestic airports by 2015, which is far less than that of the unit land area in the US or India. In this sense, the overall load factor in China is expected to rise in the future. Further, increases in aviation fuel costs should force continuous improvements in air traffic control systems and airline fleet planning, which will result in a rise in the overall load factor. Unfortunately, imbalances between western and eastern China, income gaps and high-speed railway network expansion may result in surplus airport capacity. In the long term, all these problems will be settled, prompting the overall load factor to rise. According to the growth rate of the overall load factor over the last two years in China and the historic growth rate in developed countries such as the US and Japan, we assume an annual growth rate of 0.5 per cent.

However, it is expected that technological advancements will gradually slow down. In accordance with the technological treatment of the traditional production function, the time logarithmic value is used to express and calculate the technological advancement trends. Thus, a time logarithmic value extension is used to directly express technical progress.

The first core effect factor in aviation total turnover is urbanization rate. According to the 12th Five-Year Plan, the urbanization rate in 2015 is expected to be more than 54 per cent. By the end of the first year (2011) of the 12th Five-Year Plan, the urbanization rate had reached 51.27 per cent. After the 18th CPC National Congress, the Chinese government declared that it will devote itself to narrowing the gap between rich and poor and to maintaining sustainable development. Urbanization is one important way to achieve these two goals. Therefore, urbanization is not expected to slow down in the future. According to estimates by most population experts, the urbanization rate in 2020 is predicted to exceed 60 per cent. Based on this estimation, the annual urbanization growth rate is expected to be more than 2 per cent. Here, we determine the urbanization rate from 2012 to 2020 to be a 2 per cent annual growth. These details are shown in Table 4.10.

According to the 11th Five-Year Plan and projections for 2020 issued by the State Council General Office, the population target is around 1.45 billion. General Secretary Hu Jintao stated at 18th National CPC Congress that both GDP and residents income per capita in towns and countryside in 2020 will be double that of 2010. In view of this, the annual per capita GDP from 2010 to 2020 is shown in Table 4.10.

In this chapter, before the multivariate forecast analysis for aviation fuel efficiency and aviation total turnover was conducted, a preliminary simple regression analysis for the dependent variables and the core effect factors was first conducted. The findings showed that both models and their variable coefficients were effective when an intercept term exists. Further, both the independence and the steady series residual errors showed that these factors were sufficient for the analysis. A simple regression model and a scenario predictive value can be directly used to forecast aviation fuel efficiency and aviation total turnover. However, the sample estimates had only 30 items of data and a low freedom degree. Within such models, small sample assessment can cause big errors because of the greater uncertainty. Therefore, here, we use Bayesian statistical technique, which is suitable for small samples, to assess the regression model. According to the data from the *China Statistical Yearbooks* from 1979 to 2011 (annual data), and with the assistance of WinBUGS software, the parameter estimation value for the simple regression analysis acts as the starting value for the relevant solve-for parameter in the Bayesian regression model. Ten thousand iterations were performed: the first 5,000 iterations acted as the test sample, and the second 5,000 iterations acted as the assessment sample. With a prerequisite of fine convergence and normality, this chapter presents the assessment results for the two Bayesian regression models.

1   Bayesian regression models for overall load factor (OL) and technological advancement (TA) versus aviation fuel efficiency (AFE) are calculated with Equation 4.10.

$$\ln AFE = -0.387 - 0.830 \ln OL - 0.317 \ln TA \qquad (4.10)$$

2   Bayesian regression models for urbanization rate (UR) and per capita GDP (GDP) versus air transport total turnover (ATTT) are calculated with Equation 4.10.

$$\ln ATTT = -7.672 + 3.815 \ln UR + 0.477 \ln GDP \qquad (4.11)$$

Equations 4.10 and 4.11 give the multivariate Bayesian regression analysis models for two variables. These models are both multivariate elasticity analysis models because both have the prerequisite of taking logarithmic values. Equation 4.10 shows that aviation fuel efficiency can rise by 0.8 per cent with every 1 per cent rise in the overall load factor. Equation 4.11 shows that aviation total turnover can rise by 3.8 per cent with a 1 per cent rise in the urbanization rate and by 0.4 per cent with every 1 per cent rise in the per capita GDP. In combination with the future baseline scenario analysis in Table 4.10, using the results shown in Equations 4.10 and 4.11, we are able to determine the predictive values for aviation total turnover, aviation fuel efficiency and aviation fuel demand from 2012 to 2020, as shown in Table 4.11.

Table 4.12 shows that the synthesis forecast value for the time series technology is larger than that of the Bayesian multivariate regression under a scenario

Table 4.11 Forecasting results for the Bayesian model for aviation fuel demand

	Parameter	AFE	ATTT	AFD
Forecasting result	2012	0.288	68156.810	1964.992
	2013	0.285	75918.340	2160.364
	2014	0.281	84563.740	2375.741
	2015	0.277	94193.660	2613.195
	2016	0.274	104920.200	2875.013
	2017	0.271	116868.300	3163.722
	2018	0.267	130176.900	3482.113
	2019	0.264	145001.200	3833.268
	2020	0.261	161513.600	4220.593

Note: AFD, aviation fuel demand (10,000 tons); AFE, aviation fuel efficiency (kg/ ton-km); and ATTT, aviation transport total turnover (megaton km)

Table 4.12 Forecasting results for aviation fuel demand (AFD, 10,000 tons)

Model	ETS	ARIMA	Multivariate Bayesian regression model	Combination forecast in model
2012	1963.704	1859.095	1964.992	1964.348
2013	2229.362	2074.387	2160.364	2194.863
2014	2532.451	2314.632	2375.741	2454.096
2015	2878.288	2582.703	2613.195	2745.742
2016	3273.045	2881.793	2875.013	3074.029
2017	3723.792	3215.551	3163.722	3443.757
2018	4238.526	3587.963	3482.113	3860.32
2019	4826.505	4003.503	3833.268	4329.887
2020	5498.359	4467.128	4220.593	4859.476
Annual growth rate	12.968 per cent	10.421 per cent	9.6798 per cent	11.4186 per cent

analysis. In other words, if historic development trends remain unchanged, aviation fuel demand will grow significantly. Furthermore, the forecast results for the two time series models are somewhat different. As mentioned in Section 4.4.1, the ARIMA model appears to be theoretically optimal for aviation fuel efficiency forecasting, but the ETS forecast for aviation fuel efficiency is much closer to the historic data and theoretical expectations. Thus, the ETS was chosen as the time series model. The Bayesian multivariate regression forecast takes account of the changing trends in the core effect factors in the decomposition index. When a baseline scenario is set, the forecast value for aviation fuel efficiency obtained from this model is similar to that from the ETS time series model. However, the forecast results for air transport total turnover in these two models are quite different. This is mainly because the government program believes that growth rate of urbanization rate and per capita income will eventually slow down. Even if the historic development trend is maintained, the growth rate will fall. This sounds theoretically reasonable and makes the multivariate forecast results less than those from the time series model under historical memorability rules. The multivariate model was also obtained from historical data and extends the relationship between variables to forecasting. This model actually has the memorability of a univariate time series recursion model and uses current information to pre-estimate and amend the forecast.

Many factors that have not been considered may have important effects in the future, such as airport expansions, the consumption conception's change and most importantly efficiency. It is likely that such factors may eliminate the unfavorable influences caused by the core effect factors selected by this chapter. Thus, the univariate time series recursion model and the Bayesian multivariate regression model have their own advantages and disadvantages. Combined forecasts are also considered in this chapter. Weight selection for combined forecasts has been discussed in many articles (Kurz-Kim, 2008). However, different models have their own advantages and disadvantages. When combined, giving different weights requires a sequencing of the models by superiority or inferiority. So, here, we do not proceed with combinations. A better method is to select an optimal model, as with such as model, the simple equal weight combined forecast model shows sound justifiability and applicability. Based on these factors, this chapter uses an ETS model and a multivariate Bayesian regression model to conduct an equal weight combined forecast. For detailed computation solutions, see Table 4.12.

4.5 Conclusions

China became the second largest aviation fuel consumer in 2011, resulting in greater international pressure for environmental protection. Oil price rises pushed fuel costs upward, leading to increased costs for airline companies. In this chapter, we presented an analysis and forecast for future aviation fuel demand through an analysis of the core influencing factors, thus providing meaningful insights into fuel cost control and offering guidance on the selection of risk-related decisions in advance. Further, this analysis could be useful as a government reference for the development of policies for a green aviation fuel industry, aviation fuel imports and exports and oil refinery investments.

Previous research on aviation fuel demand analysis or forecasts generally focused on forecasting aviation fuel demand, rather than investigating changes in aviation fuel consumption, aviation fuel costs and aviation fuel efficiency, all of which can affect aviation fuel demand to 2020 in China.

In view of these important implications for aviation enterprise cost control through this analysis and forecast, we focused on the aviation fuel consumption structure for our decomposition analysis, not only by analyzing the core factors and aviation fuel consumption impact path in China, but also by conducting a structural decomposition analysis for aviation fuel consumption cost changes and increases in the main business profit in aviation enterprises.

The conclusions of this study are as follows:

1   Technological advancements are the main factor, and the aviation load factor is the main restrictive factor, in aviation fuel efficiency improvements. In addition, the aviation load factor fluctuation was found to have an important influence on aviation fuel efficiency fluctuations. Long-term fuel efficiency and technological advancements trends were found to have a significant correlation.
2   The urbanization rate was found to promote air transport consumption demand, which is in agreement with conclusions in previous studies. Further, the long-term aviation total turnover trend was found to have a significant correlation with the urbanization rate and the real per capita GDP, which indicates that the long-term aviation total turnover trend is influenced greatly by macroeconomic developments and changes in population structure.
3   Aviation fuel costs from 1997 to 2010 declined in 1998, 2001 and 2009 because of the lower aviation fuel prices in 1998 and because of the enhanced efficiency and lower aviation fuel prices in 2001 and 2009. A rising CPI and aviation fuel price was found to lead to rising costs and declining profits for aviation enterprises. Further, cost reductions due to technological advancements were not found to offset the cost of owning and/or operating airplanes. Therefore, under the current circumstances, increasing main business profits depends on increasing the total turnover in China.

This chapter resolved aviation fuel demand into an efficiency factor and a total quantity factor, namely aviation fuel efficiency and air transport total turnover, and thoroughly analyzed these two indexes. The findings demonstrated that aviation fuel efficiency is expected to continue to improve, but as air transport total turnover rapidly increases, total aviation fuel demand also is expected to increase. By the end of the 12th Five-Year Plan, aviation fuel demand in China is predicted to be close to 28 million tons and will be 50 million tons by 2020. The annual average aviation fuel demand growth rate from 2012 to 2020 is expected to reach 11.4 per cent. Based on this forecast and analysis, we propose the following:

1   For enterprises, ever-increasing aviation fuel demand means that fuel costs are an important component of running costs. Under such circumstances, adjustments in cost control strategies following oil price fluctuations are important. The fluctuation in aviation fuel prices results in changes to the running cost structure for airline companies, influencing stability. In the past few years, for Air China, the steady rise in global aviation fuel prices has pushed the fuel costs upward, with the proportion of running costs climbing to 41 per cent from 33 per cent, which has reduced profits and increased cost pressures. These aviation fuel cost pressures may remain unchanged in the future. Oil prices were relatively high in 2011, and many airline companies chose to use fuel hedging. China has now preliminarily established

such mechanisms to reduce the risks resulting from oil price rises. Three linkages between oil prices and fuel surcharges have been established. The fuel surcharge charging rights are transferred to the airline companies from competent departments. The airline companies have improved their ability to independently control costs. Fuel surcharges have become a steady source of income for airline companies because these are not influenced by passenger ticket discounts and the ability to implement these surcharges quickly and effectively greatly improves the ability to stabilize oil price fluctuations. When the oil price remains high, fuel hedging is an effective measure to control costs. However, when oil price falls, the cost advantages of this disappears and hedging can mean higher costs for airlines. Therefore, with the ever-increasing aviation fuel demand, airlines need to diagnose oil price trends according to macro policy and economic fundamentals and then take such measures as the timely adjustment of ticket prices, improving fuel service efficiencies, becoming involved in hedging and collecting fuel surcharges as well as adjusting management and cost control strategies.

2   The civil aviation industry is closely linked with economic and social development, people's livelihoods and state security. Since the reform and opening up of China, the civil aviation industry has developed at a rate of 17.6 per cent in China, which is far higher than any other mode of transport. Starting in 2005, China has become the second largest aviation transport country. According to the forecasts in this chapter, civil aviation transport total turnover in 2020 is expected to reach 181.11 billion tons/km. At the same time, aviation fuel demand will continue to grow. Based on the forecasts in this chapter, aviation fuel demand is expected to exceed 48 million tons in 2020, which will put great pressure on traditional aviation fuel supply security. However, there is a good opportunity for green aviation fuel development as around 3.14 tons of carbon dioxide is generated by 1 ton of aviation fuel demand. The global "carbon countermeasure", initiated by the EU carbon tax, brings great challenges to aviation fuel demand and the sustainable development of the civil aviation industry in China, but it assists with carbon emissions trading market development. Therefore, the rapid development of green fuel and the establishment of a carbon emissions trading system are of great importance for China to maintain sustainable civil aviation competitive power.

5 Comparative analysis of asymmetric price effects on traffic demand

5.1 Introduction

The *Blue Book of World Energy: Annual Development Report on World Energy* (2013) points out that China will become the greatest contributor to oil consumption growth and will replace the US as the world largest oil consumer. The main sources of oil consumption growth of China are the industrial and transportation sectors. With decreasing energy consumption and slower population increase in the process of industrial development, the transportation industry will become the main driving force of growth of oil consumption. On the one hand, oil is regarded as "blood of modern industry", and oil consumption can drive economic growth in China (Zou et al., 2006); on the other hand, oil consumption will cause environmental degradation. Among all oil products, the output of fuel materials including gasoline, diesel, jet fuel and fuel oil is the largest, about 90 per cent of the total output of oil products. The impact of oil consumption on the environment is mainly from emissions from the mass use of liquid fuel such as CO, CO_2, HC and NO_x. With the deepening progress of industrialization and urbanization, China's environment will face great pollution pressure caused by continuous consumption of oil products in the transportation sector. As the driving force of oil products consumption in the transportation sector, transportation demand is negatively correlated with oil price. When the prices rise, demand will fall (Litman, 2011). Price is the major means regulating supply and demand and the main method to alleviate the current pressure of pollution caused by transportation.

Domestic and foreign scholars have conducted numerous empirical studies on the relationship between traffic demand and price. For example, Small and Van Dender (2007) analyzed the influence of energy price on traffic demand and pointed out that, for all countries, especially developing countries like China, continuous increase of traffic demand is one of the main causes of oil price rise. However, there is certain impact of population and income: relatively high prices do not drive down traffic demand. Moreover, with increase of people's income, the influence of energy prices on traffic demand will get smaller; Kennedy and Wallis (2007) analyzed the influence of fuel price on the transportation of New Zealand and found that change in fuel price has little impact on public traffic demand, and its influence on the traffic demand in urban areas is greater than in rural areas. Its influence on the urban traffic demand during off-peak periods is greater than that during rush hours. Musso et al. (2013) studied the price elasticity of traffic demand and pointed out that rising fuel prices will result increases in price elasticity; Thomas Sterner highlighted the importance of fuel duties and held that the short-term price elasticity of fuel is low and the long-term elasticity is relatively large, which is significant for policy formulation.

Though existing studies have analyzed the relationship between traffic demand and price from various aspects, only a few of them focus on the asymmetric influence of the price on traffic demand. Traditionally, the demand models are built based on the implicit assumption that the response of demand on price rise and fall are symmetric. However, traffic demand, as the driving force of oil consumption in the transportation sector, includes demands of gasoline and diesel. Moreover, irreversible technological progress, price expectations and the existence of fixed costs are some factors causing the asymmetric price effects. Rising oil prices will also promote fuel efficiency enhancements and further stipulate traffic demand. So the influence of oil price on the traffic demand might be asymmetric. The purpose of this study is to test this statistical hypothesis. This chapter will decompose gasoline price and diesel price and build up a Koyck infinite distributed lag model to compare and analyze asymmetric effect of the price of oil products in China, Japan and the US from two perspectives: passenger transport demand and freight transport demand. This chapter mainly focuses on the asymmetric influence of oil price on the traffic demand.

5.2 Model building

The short-term influence of oil price on the traffic demand embodies such aspects as modes of transportation and running routes. However, the long-term influence manifests in the aspects of selection of work and home address, ownership of vehicles, land use and so on. In this chapter, we will establish a simple linear equation to analyze the influence of current price on traffic demand; moreover, we will build up a Koyck geometric distributed lag model to analyze the influence of prices at present and in the past on the traffic demand. Moreover, this chapter adopts a price decomposition model to decompose the price variables in the simple linear and Koyck geometric distributed lag models and further discusses the influence of rising and falling prices on traffic demand.

5.2.1 Koyck geometric distributed lag model

The Koyck geometric distributed lag model is the most popular structured infinite distributed lag model and has been widely used in the studies on the long-term regulation relationship between energy demand and energy price (e.g. Hogan, 1993; Gately, 2002; Griffin and Schulman, 2005 etc.). The basic assumption of this model is that, with increase of the number of lag phase, the influence of the lagged variable on the explanatory variable will get smaller and smaller.

As shown in Equation 5.1, the influence of the lagged explanatory variable Υ_{t-i} on the explained variable Z will be weakened in geometrical progression with increase of the number of lagged phase i.

$$Z_t = k + \beta P_t + \beta \lambda P_{t-1} + \beta \lambda^2 P_{t-2} + \ldots + \varepsilon_t \tag{5.1}$$

Hereinto, Z_t represents the turnover in phase t, P_t represents the price in phase t and ε_t is the error term. Equation 5.2 shows what happens when there is a 1-phase lag applied to Equation 5.1.

$$Z_{t-1} = k + \beta P_{t-1} + \beta \lambda P_{t-2} + \beta \lambda^2 P_{t-3} + \ldots + \varepsilon_{t-1} \tag{5.2}$$

Equation 5.3 shows the Koyck conversion, i.e. Equation 5.1 minus the λ of Equation 5.2.

$$Z_t = k_1 + \beta_1 P_t + \lambda Z_{t-1} + \mu_t \tag{5.3}$$

Hereinto $k_1 = k(1 - \lambda); \beta_1 = \beta(1 - \lambda); \mu_t = \varepsilon_t - \lambda \varepsilon_{t-1}$, by Koyck conversion, the lagged explanatory variable is converted to Z_{t-1} DOF (degree of freedom) of the model is enhanced; the problem of confirming the number of lag phases is solved; multicollinearity of the model is alleviated. However, after conversion, the error term μ_t is relevant to μ_{t-1} and Z_{t-1} and $\text{cov}(\mu_t, \mu_{t-1}) \neq 0$. When $\text{cov}(\mu t, Z_{t-1}) \neq 0$, the ordinary least square estimation (OLS) is a biased estimate. When μ_t is relevant to Z_{t-1}, the instrumental variable method can be used to find the correlation between the explained variable and the random disturbance term. When μ_t is relevant to μ_{t-1} and the random disturbance term has autocorrelation, the generalized least squares method can be used to remove this correlation.

5.2.2 Price decomposition model

Price decomposition models were originally proposed by Wolffram (1971), and he decomposed price into two parts: rise and fall. Traill et al. (1978) decomposed price into the greatest price fluctuation and other minor changes. Dargay and Gately (1997) were the first to decompose price fluctuation into the historical highest price, restored price and falling price, namely P_{max}, P_{rec} and P_{cut}. Many domestic and foreign scholars like Gately (1992), Hogan (1993), Dargay and Gately (1997) and Kong (2010) have studied asymmetric effects on fuel demand for transportation through price decomposition. Gately (1992) pointed out that oil consumption responses to falling prices is smaller than that when prices are rising, and Dargay and Gately (1997) mentioned that consumers' responses to rising and falling prices are different and that the symmetric demand model will create derivative elasticity estimations. Kong (2010) discussed asymmetric price effects of coal consumption of China. Sentenac-Chemin (2012) found that, in India, an emerging country, price fluctuation has no asymmetric influence on gasoline consumption. Griffin and Schulman (2005) held that development of energy saving technologies leads to asymmetric price effects on oil demand and pointed out that the asymmetric price model relies on the data origination stage. Walker and Wirl (1993) mentioned that the irreversibility of technological progress, price expectations and the existence of fixed costs are some factors causing the asymmetric effect of price. Rising oil prices will also promote enhancement of fuel efficiency and further stipulate traffic demand. The transportation industry is a main oil-consuming sector. Traffic demand includes demands of gasoline and diesel, so the influence of changes in gasoline prices and diesel prices on traffic demand may also be asymmetric.

In order to distinguish the influences of rising and falling prices on traffic demand, this chapter decomposes the price of the refined oil products into the accumulative increase in the highest historical price range, the accumulative segment increase and accumulative price decrease. The specific decomposition formula is shown in Equation 5.4.

$$P_t = P_1 + P_{max,t} + P_{rec,t} + P_{cut,t} \tag{5.4}$$

$$\left\{ \begin{array}{l} P_{max,t} = \max\{0, (P_2 - P_1)...(P_t \text{-} P_1)\} \ (5.5) \\[2mm] P_{rec,t} = \displaystyle\sum_{i=1}^{t} \max\{0, [P_{max,i-1} - (P_{i-1} \text{-} P_1)] - [P_{max,i} - (P_i \text{-} P_1)]\} \ (5.6) \\[2mm] P_{cut,t} = \displaystyle\sum_{i=1}^{t} \min\{0, [P_{max,i-1} - (P_{i-1} - P_1)] - [P_{max,i} - (P_i - P_1)]\} \ (5.7) \end{array} \right.$$

P_1 represents the initial price of the refined oil product. P_{max} represents the highest historical price sequence decomposed from the price sequences of the refined oil price and is used to express fluctuation of the highest historical price of the refined oil product. P_{rec} represents price recovery sequence of the refined oil product decomposed from the price sequences of the refined oil price and is used to express the price rise process, and P_{cut} represents price decreasing sequence decomposed from the price sequences of the refined oil price and is used to express the process of falling prices.

In this chapter, we will use a simple linear model, an infinite distributed lag model, a simple linear model after price decomposition and a Koyck infinite lag model after price decomposition for empirical analysis, as follows:

① Simple linear equation

$$Z_t = k + \beta P_t + \mu_t \tag{5.5}$$

② Geometric distributed lag model

$$Z_t = k + \beta P_t + \beta\lambda P_{t-1} + \beta\lambda^2 P_{t-2} + ... + \varepsilon_t \tag{5.6}$$

Koyck converted to:

$$Z_t = k_1 + \beta P_t + \lambda Z_{t-1} \tag{5.7}$$

③ Simple linear model after price decomposition

$$Z_t = k + \beta_m P_{\max,t} + \beta_r P_{rec,t} + \beta_c P_{cut,t} + \mu_t \tag{5.8}$$

④ Infinite lag model after price decomposition

$$Z_t = k + \beta_m P_{\max,t} + \beta_r P_{rec,t} + \beta_c P_{cut,t} + \lambda Z_{t-1} \tag{5.9}$$

5.3 Empirical analysis

5.3.1 Data dedication

In this chapter, we divide traffic demand into freight transport demand and passenger transport demand based on the object. As traffic turnover is "the weight of cargo (or the number of passengers) × distance" and includes two elements of the traffic demand, namely flow and process, we take traffic turnover as the index to measure the traffic demand. In this analysis, such indexes are gasoline price, diesel price, passenger transport turnover and freight transport turnover. Compared with the wholesale price, the retail price of the refined oil product can better embody the regulating effect of the pricing mechanism, so we will take gasoline and diesel retail prices in each country in this study. Considering availability of data, this chapter uses 2010–2012 monthly data from China and Japan and 1990–2013 annual data from the US. The Chinese data all comes from the China National Bureau of Statistics; the American data, from the Energy Information Administration and the Bureau of Transportation Statistics; and the Japanese data, from the Bureau of Statistics of Japan and the Ministry of Land Infrastructure and Transport. In order to remove multicollinearity, when making empirical analysis in this chapter, we will use logarithmic processes toward all index data in the models.

5.3.2 Comparative analysis on oil prices in China, Japan and the US

This chapter decomposes and compares the monthly oil price data (gasoline and diesel) of China, Japan and the US from 2010 to 2012 (see Figure 5.1). Firstly, Japan's oil prices are the highest. The second highest is China, and the lowest is the US. Oil prices depend on public policy orientation. Japan adopts a high-oil-price policy, while the US adopts a low-oil-price policy. The refined oil tax rate is the main factor causing the price difference among the three countries. In the oil price structure of Japan, tax revenue takes up about 40 per cent. The government controls refined oil consumption through taxation; in China, oil price is composed of consumption tax, value-added tax, urban maintenance and construction

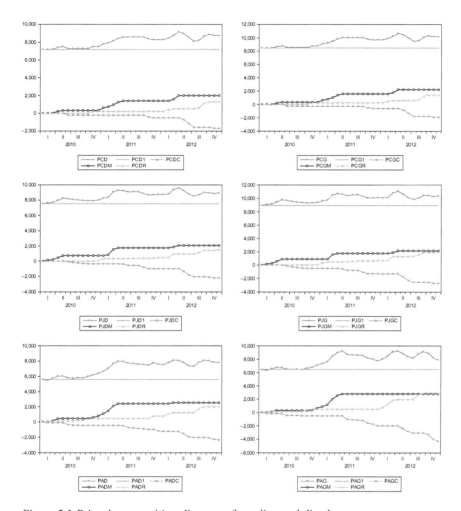

Figure 5.1 Price decomposition diagram of gasoline and diesel

Note: PCD, diesel price in China; PCG, gasoline price in China; PJD, diesel price in Japan; PJG, gasoline price in Japan; PAD diesel price in the US; and PAG gasoline price in Japan.

tax, educational surcharge, tariff etc. The total tax rate is about 30 per cent; the US has adopted a fixed-amount tax, and the ratio of tax revenue is about 12 per cent. Secondly, a comparison is made by combining the recovery prices and the declining prices of gasoline and diesel of each country after price decomposition. Recovery price P_{rec} and declining price P_{cut} form a V-shape opening. The extent of the opening can be interpreted into minor increases or decreases in price (small fluctuations). The larger the opening is, the greater the fluctuation will be. It can be found that oil price fluctuation of the US is the largest; Japan is the second largest, and China ranks third.

As shown in Figure 5.1, there were three large crests in the US oil price curve in May 2011, April 2012 and September 2012. The price fluctuation is relatively violent, but the fluctuations occur in low prices. The oil price curve of Japan also has three crests, in May 2010, April 2011 and April 2012. But the fluctuation is smaller than that of the US; as for the curve of China, there is only one obvious crest in April 2012. Before that, the curve is smooth and has no peak value. In Japan and the US, the refined oil price is formed in market competition, and the price is completely determined by the market. However, in China, refined oil is priced by the government. From January 2010 to December 2012, the price-regulating basis of China was based on *Oil Price Control Measures* issued by the National Development and Reform Commission (NDRC) in May 2009. It stipulates that, when the fluctuation range of the moving average price of crude oil on the international market surpasses 4 per cent, the domestic refined oil price can be regulated accordingly. China only has one crest synchronizing with the US and Japan, which shows that the deepening reform of refined oil price-regulating methods is now driving the Chinese refined oil market docking with the international platform, as China gradually realized marketization. As the oil price of the US is totally determined by the market, when comparing the oil price of China with that of the US, we find that, from September 2010 to May 2011, American oil price rose significantly. Correspondingly, Chinese oil prices also increased sharply from October 2010 to May 2011, but the amount of rise was smaller than that of the US. From May 2011 to December 2011, American oil prices declined sharply. However, Chinese oil prices were stable from May 2011 to September 2011 and only fell a little from September 2011 to December 2011. It highlights the problems of "more rise and less fall" and the response lag caused by the NDRC's longstanding policy of delayed and inadequate oil price regulation. Furthermore, by comparing the historical highest gasoline and diesel prices of the three countries, we find that the P_{max} of the US and China had a large long-term rise from November 2010 to April 2011. However, during this period, Japan only had a small increase from January 2011 to April 2011. This might be because, after 2008 international financial crisis, the world economy showed satisfactory recovery during that period, and both the US and China have promising economic states. In addition, oil price increases might also be driven by the cold climate in the northern hemisphere.

5.3.3 Asymmetric price effect of the passenger transport demand

Passenger transport demand of China

Table 5.1 shows the regression results of gasoline and diesel toward passenger transport demand of China. Hereinto, the long-term price elasticity is calculated by $\beta_n / (1-\lambda)$. Among equations of gasoline price, according to the model's goodness of fit, we determine Equation ④ is optimal. So the relation of absolute values of the coefficients is $\beta_m < \beta_c < \beta_y$. It shows that the influence of the rise process of price recovery on the passenger transport demand is the greatest.

Table 5.1 Result of Chinese passenger transport

Type of the refined oil product	Equation	Coefficient				Lag coefficient	Long-term price elasticity
		β	βm	βr	βc	λ	ξ
Gasoline	①	1.0					
	②	0.23				0.68	0.67
	③		0.63	−0.43	−0.75		
	④		0.41	−0.65	−0.75	0.32	0.81
Diesel	①	0.97					
	②	0.21				0.68	0.54
	③		0.65	−0.36	−0.67		
	④		0.39	−0.58	−0.69	0.35	0.81

Moreover, Wald test results refute the original assumption that $\beta_m < \beta_Y < \beta_C$ and prove that fluctuation of gasoline price has an asymmetric influence on the passenger transport demand. Among equations of diesel, according to the model's goodness of fit, we determine Equation ③ is optimal. So the relation among absolute values of the coefficients is $\beta_C < \beta_m < \beta_Y$. It is commonly recognized that oil price is negatively related to the traffic demand (Zou et al., 2006). But the results of Equation ③ on gasoline price and Equation ④ on diesel price, after price decomposition, are different from our expectations. From the two equations, β_m is positive, which shows that, when the price is higher than the historical highest price and keeps rising, the traffic demand will increase. In China, oil price is not determined by the market, and it is widely recognized that Chinese oil price always rises and seldom falls. When price reaches record highs, people will believe that the price will continue rising but will not fall, so they will buy oil in advance. According to Table 5.1, price elasticity is 0.35 and 0.81, which shows that Chinese passenger transport demand is inelastic to oil price fluctuations, and the two are in positive correlation. As David Kennedy (2007) has mentioned, high oil prices do not result in decreases in traffic demand in China.

Passenger transport demand of the US

Table 5.2 shows the regression results of gasoline price and diesel price toward passenger turnover in the US. In Equation ①, coefficient β is positive. After taking the influence of the early-stage prices into consideration, in Equation ②, β becomes negative. It shows that oil price is positive correlation with the passenger transport demand in the short term and in negative correlation in the long term. Among the equations of gasoline price, according to the model's goodness of fit, we believe Equation ③ is optimal. β_r and β_c pass the significance test. Moreover, $\beta_r > \beta_c$, which means that the influence of price rise is larger than that of price fall on the passenger transport demand. The other evidence of price asymmetry is that the Wald test refutes the original assumption that $\beta_m = \beta_Y = \beta_C$. Among the equations of diesel price, as in Equation ④, only β_C fails to pass the test; thus,

Table 5.2 Passenger transport demand of the US

Type of the refined oil product	Equation	Coefficient				Lag coefficient	Long-term price elasticity
		β	βm	βr	βc	λ	ξ
Gasoline	①	0.53					
	②	−0.03				0.99	−3
	③		−0.04	0.44	−0.33		
	④		−0.06	0.03	0.02	1.00	−0.06
Diesel	①	0.45					
	②	−0.02				0.99	−2
	③		0.005	0.53	−0.05		
	④		−0.04	0.10	0.04	0.93	−0.57

we believe Equation ④ is optimal: $\beta_\gamma > \beta_n$. The Wald test refutes the original assumption that $\beta_m = \beta_\gamma = \beta_C$. At this time, β_m is negative, and β_γ is positive.

5.3.4 Asymmetric price effect of the freight transport demand

Freight transport demand of China

Table 5.3 shows the regression results of gasoline price and diesel price toward passenger turnover of China. Regardless of which gasoline or diesel price equation is used, price elasticity is greater than 1. Compared with passenger transport demand, freight transport demand is more sensitive to price fluctuation of gasoline and diesel. Among equations of gasoline price, according to the model's goodness of fit, we determine Equation ④ is optimal. Here, the results of the Wald test cannot refute the original assumption that $\beta_m = \beta_\gamma = \beta_C$. Among equations of diesel price, according to the model's goodness of fit, we determine Equation ④ is optimal. Evidence exists showing the asymmetric influence of fluctuation of diesel price on the freight transport demand. The results of the Wald test refutes the original assumption that $\beta_m = \beta_\gamma = \beta_C$. By comparing long-term price elasticity of Equation ④ for both gasoline and diesel, we find that price elasticity of freight transport demand is positive. However, compared with the passenger transport demand, freight transport demand has greater price elasticity. It shows that freight transport demand is more sensitive to gasoline and diesel price fluctuations.

Freight transport demand of Japan

Table 5.4 shows the regression results of gasoline price and diesel price toward passenger turnover of Japan. Among equations of gasoline price, according to the model's goodness of fit, we determine Equation ④ is optimal. Here, the results of the Wald test cannot refute the original assumption that $\beta_m = \beta_\gamma = \beta_C$. At this time, long-term price elasticity of freight transport demand is −1.64. Among

Table 5.3 Result of Chinese freight transport demand

Type of the refined oil product	Equation	Coefficient				Lag coefficient	Long-term price elasticity
		β	βm	βr	βc	λ	ξ
Gasoline	①	1.36					
	②	0.91				0.31	1.45
	③		0.87	0.40	−0.10		
	④		0.73	0.44	−0.05	0.10	1.11
Diesel	①	1.32					
	②	0.88				0.31	1.42
	③		1.02	0.41	−0.02		
	④		0.89	0.43	0.01	0.09	1.23

Table 5.4 Result of Japanese freight transport demand

Type of the refined oil product	Equation	Coefficient				Lag coefficient	Long-term price elasticity
		β	βm	βr	βc	λ	ξ
Gasoline	①	−1.52					
	②	−0.98				0.41	−1.67
	③		−1.47	−0.3	−0.24		
	④		−1.38	−0.25	−0.27	0.16	−1.64
Diesel	①	−1.35					
	②	−0.93				0.36	−1.45
	③		−1.17	−0.36	−0.22		
	④		−1.09	−0.36	−0.29	0.17	−6.4

equations of diesel price, according to the model's goodness of fit, we determine Equation ④ is optimal. Here, the results of the Wald test cannot refute the original assumption that $\beta_m = \beta_\gamma = \beta_C$. At this time, long-term price elasticity of freight transport demand is –6.4. It cannot be judged whether the influence of fluctuation of diesel price on the freight transport demand is asymmetric. Both short-term and long-term price elasticity are less than –1, which shows that in Japan, elasticity of price fluctuation of gasoline and diesel toward freight transport demand is high.

Freight transport demand of the US

Table 5.5 shows the regression results of gasoline price and diesel price toward passenger turnover in the US. Among equations of gasoline price, according to the model's goodness of fit, we determine Equation ③ is optimal. Here, the relation of absolute values of the gasoline price coefficients after decomposition is $\beta_m > \beta_C > \beta_\gamma$. The Wald test results refute the original assumption that $\beta_m = \beta_\gamma = \beta_C$. Among equations of diesel price, according to the model's goodness of fit, we determine

Table 5.5 Result of American freight transport demand

Type of the refined oil product	Equation	Coefficient				Lag coefficient	Long-term price elasticity
		β	βm	βr	βc	λ	ξ
Gasoline	(1)	0.15					
	(2)	0.06				0.55	−1.5
	(3)		0.14	0.11	0.09		
	(4)		0.04	0.17	0.17	0.68	−0.81
Diesel	(1)	0.13					
	(2)	0.07				0.47	−0.67
	(3)		0.13	0.13	0.13		
	(4)		0.04	0.16	0.15	0.61	2.5

Equation ③ is optimal. Here, the relation of absolute values of the diesel price coefficients after decomposition is $\beta_C > \beta_m > \beta_Y$. The Wald test refutes the original assumption that $\beta_m = \beta_Y = \beta_C$. In the two optimal equations, β_m is negative, β_Y is positive and β_C is negative.

5.4 Conclusion

In this chapter, we established a Koyck distributed lag model, based on comparison and analysis of gasoline and diesel prices of China, Japan and the US, to discuss the long-term influence of gasoline and diesel prices on the passenger transport demand and the freight transport demand. Furthermore, depending on the price decomposition model, this chapter analyzed the asymmetric influences of the historical highest price, price recovery and price fall on passenger transport demand and freight transport demand. Traditionally, demand models are built based on the implicit assumption that the response of demand on price rise and fall are symmetric.

As for China, gasoline and diesel price levels are between the US and Japan, and fluctuations in gasoline price and diesel prices are the smallest, except for the asymmetric influence of gasoline price fluctuations on freight transport demand, which cannot be proven. The asymmetric effects of other items all have evidence of support; gasoline and diesel prices are positively related to traffic demand (passenger transport demand and freight transport demand). Traffic demand does not decrease with increases in oil price. Moreover, freight transport demand is more sensitive to price fluctuation than passenger transport demand; the historical highest prices of gasoline and diesel are in positive correlation with traffic demand. When the price is higher than the historical highest price and keeps rising, traffic demand will increase. This phenomenon is caused by the irrational expectations of Chinese consumers and based on their observations that Chinese oil prices often rise but seldom fall. Regarding Japan, the price levels of both gasoline and diesel are the highest among the three countries, while price fluctuations of gasoline and diesel are between China and the US. Both fluctuations of gasoline price and diesel price have an asymmetric influence on passenger trans-port demand. However, the fit coefficient of the regression model is unsatisfac-tory, which shows that influences of gasoline and diesel prices on the passenger transport demand are small. Speaking of the US, both gasoline price and diesel price are the lowest. But the fluctuations are the greatest: in the US, price fluc-tuations of gasoline and diesel have asymmetric influences on both passenger transport demand and freight transport demand; the long-term relation between gasoline and diesel prices and the traffic demand (passenger transport demand and freight transport demand) is negative. And freight transport demand is more sensitive to price fluctuation than passenger transport demand; the price recovery process is positively correlated to the traffic demand (passenger transport demand and freight transport demand), because American oil prices are totally deter-mined by the market. The range and frequency of gasoline diesel price fluctua-tions are the largest among the three countries. When gasoline and diesel prices are lower than the historical high price levels and are on the rise, both passenger transport demand and freight transport demand will increase. American consum-ers who know historical price levels will expect that prices will rise in future. So they consume in advance (e.g. advancing their travel plans).

As transportation becomes the largest oil-consuming sector in China, how to control traffic demand by regulating the refined oil price to alleviate the pressure of environment pollution creased from transportation becomes a hard issue. In this chapter, we found that, in market-oriented countries like Japan and the US, traffic demand is in negative relation with oil price. As refined oil price is set by the government in China, consumers have irrational expectations. In China, traf-fic demand is positively related to oil price. So it is hard to alleviate the pressure of environmental pollution brought by the transportation sector by raising the refined oil price. However, the problem of energy consumption and pollution by the transportation industry can be eased by the negative influence of the price recovery stage on passenger transport demand. As for freight transport, as Chi-nese economy enjoys extensive growth over a long time, freight turnover volume per unit GDP is high. The problem of excessive transport is severe. Therefore, in order to reduce the traffic demand and energy consumption and pollution by transportation, it is necessary to optimize the industrial structure and the trans-portation structure, a perspective that requires deeper study.

6 Effect of transportation structure on CO_2 emissions reduction

Because of the frequent haze that has beset Chinese cities in the last two years, emissions reduction in the transportation industry has become a top priority for China's energy and environmental strategies. On the basis of this, this chapter discusses the impact of an optimized transport structure on traffic emissions reduction. A quantitative approach and panel data (time series: 1991–2011; cross sectional samples: China, the United States, the European Union and Japan) were used to analyze the effect of transportation structures on carbon emissions. In this study, a fixed effect variable coefficient model was built by considering the road turnover per cent, railways, waterage and civil aviation and the per unit conversion CO_2 turnover emissions in the transportation industry. The empirical results showed that a rise in water transport and railway percentages would reduce traffic carbon emissions, especially in Japan and the EU. A 1 per cent increase in the proportion of Japanese transport via railway would lead to a 3.63 per cent drop in per unit conversion of CO_2 turnover emissions in the transportation industry, and a 1 per cent increase in the proportion of EU transport via water would lead to a significant carbon emissions reduction of approximately 22.11 per cent. The chapter not only extends the studies on transport structural emissions reduction from a theoretical analysis level to quantitative computation but provides a valuable reference for traffic structure optimization in China.

6.1 Introduction

With haze a continuous problem in many cities in China in the last two years, studies on energy conservation and emissions reduction in the transportation industry has become urgent. In 2013, the Institute of Atmospheric Physics, Chinese Academy of Sciences, disclosed that the exhaust gases produced by motor vehicles were the largest source of PM2.5 (particles for which the air dynamics has an equivalent diameter less than or equal to 2.5 microns) in Beijing, accounting for 20–30 per cent. Since China's reform and opening up, the transportation industry has experienced rapid improvements in traffic infrastructure and passenger-freight traffic turnover. Nowadays, highways and railways play a dominant role in China's passenger transportation industry, with 40.81 per cent and 38.43 per cent of total turnover in 2013, and waterways and highways dominate the current freight transport, with 48.21 per cent and 33.93 per cent of total turnover in 2013. This boom in transportation has been accompanied by a rapid increase in energy consumption, with China's transport energy consumption showing the highest rates of increase over the past 22 years. According to the *China Transportation Yearbook*, energy consumption had an average annual growth of 10.33 per cent from 1990–2012 (Ministry of Transport, 2013), about three times the national growth rate (3.74 per cent, according to the China Bureau of Statistics). Therefore, the carbon footprint in the transportation sector has increased rapidly in recent years. Statistics published by the *World Bank* indicated that the CO_2 emissions produced by the Chinese transport sector had risen to 623.32 million tons in 2011, compared to only 108.66 million tons in1990, an average annual growth rate of 9.19 per cent. China's greenhouse gases in the transport sector mainly arise from highways at 78.93 per cent in 2011. Therefore, structural energy conversion and emissions reduction in the transport sector is crucial at this stage to ensure the development of an environmentally friendly transport sector in China.

As the economic lifeline of a country, these transportation issues have attracted a growing body of research (Fan and Qin, 2013), which has been mainly focused on energy consumption and carbon emissions problems. Previous research has examined energy consumption structures, energy consumption measurement and calculations, low-carbon evaluation indices and suggestions on how to develop low-carbon transport (Chang et al., 2010; Liu et al., 2011; Wu et al., 2012; Zhang et al., 2012; Wang et al., 2013).

To achieve energy conservation and environmental protection by optimizing the transport structure, we need to first analyze the factors that influence traffic energy consumption and then estimate the sensitivity of the transport structure adjustment to carbon emissions reduction, so as to provide a logical foundation for the transport structural adjustment. In summarizing the research in this area, the main factors that have been identified as impacting transport emissions reduction are energy prices, technical improvements in energy saving and taxation policies.

In terms of the relationship between energy prices and emissions reduction in the transportation industry, there have been some differences between research in China and that from other countries. Wei et al. (2013) used energy price data from 1988 to 2008 to build a hierarchical regression and concluded that energy prices had a weak impact on lowering energy intensity and had little regulation effect on the transport structure, transport interdependency or technical progress in the economy. In contrast, Haldenbilen (2006) used Turkish energy price data from 1990 to 2004 to build linear exponential growth models and found that the exponential price growth mechanism could effectively reduce energy consumption.

With respect to the impact of technical progress on emissions reduction in the transportation sector, Chen and Fan (2014) established a stochastic programming model and predicted that the substitution of clean fuel for fossil fuel would have a significant impact on carbon emissions reduction from 2013 to 2020 in the state of California in the US. Based on the analysis of the current status, the environmental impact and countermeasures for greenhouse gas emissions produced by the Dutch civil aviation sector, Janić (2014) concluded that liquid hydrogen (LH) substitution for fuel oil could allow for the development of an environmentally friendly civil aviation industry. Kim and Moon (2008) utilized a scenario analysis model and concluded that the introduction of liquid hydrogen would promote energy conservation and emissions reduction in the transport sector.

Measures such as a transport tax policies and transport congestion charges have been found to be important for transport structure adjustment and fluent urban public traffic. Hofer, Dresner and Windle (2010) used a scenario analysis model and found that there would be an annual reduction in CO_2 emissions of 2.27 billion kilograms if all US airlines paid a carbon emissions tax of 2 per cent. However, about one-third of this carbon emissions cut would be offset by the increased carbon emissions coming from other transport, as demand for these services would increase as prices for the civil aviation services rose. Further, the analysis found that a high tax rate for long-distance transport and a low tax rate for short-distance transport could also minimize carbon emissions. Chunark et al. (2014), Cohen-Blankshtain (2008), Fu and Kelly (2012), Kunert and Kuhfeld (2007) examined samples from Thailand, Ireland, Israel and the EU respectively. However, Wei, Zhao and Xiao (2013) found that China's transportation system was to the left of the Kuznets curve, and it was impossible to reduce carbon emissions intensity by imposing resource and environmental taxes.

Many scholars have highlighted the impact of transport structure change on emissions reduction. Wei et al. (2014) used GDP, turnover volume of all transport sectors and the respective energy consumption in China from 1988 to 2008 to launch an empirical study and found a long-term, balanced relationship between transport structure, energy intensity and transport interdependency on the economy. The impulse response from the Vector Error Correction (VEC) model showed that an optimized transport structure was not only beneficial for lower energy intensity and transport interdependency in the economy but also could promote itself for further optimization. Further, these impacts were found to have long-term sustainability. On the basis of 30 provincial capitals' transport and energy data, Cui and Li (2014) applied a three-stage virtual frontier Data Envelopment Analysis (DEA) model and concluded that optimized transport structures and advanced management played important roles in transport energy conversion.

Through a factor analysis on traffic CO_2 emissions, Shi (2011) found that energy saving and emissions reductions in the transportation industry could be achieved using three channels: structure optimization, technological progress and management improvement. However, the transport structure in China at the moment is somewhat in disarray because of the lack of coordination between transportation planning and environmental management. Further, the technological progress that has been made in transport sector emissions reduction has also not been fully considered. Therefore, considering the demonstration effect and data availability, we collected data regarding passenger turnover, freight turnover and carbon emissions from China, the US, the EU and Japan to build a panel data model so that we can comparatively analyze the impact of transport structure change on carbon emissions in the different countries.

6.2 The international comparison of transportation structure and CO_2 emissions

From the perspective of transportation structure (Figure 6.1), the proportion of transportation modes in China has changed greatly from 1990 to 2013. The proportion of railway transportation has declined rapidly, and the proportion of road transport has increased by a large margin. The proportion of railway transportation decreased from 64.38 per cent in 1990 to 33.42 in 2013, and the proportion of road transportation increased from 17.38 per cent to 41.63 per cent. The proportion of water transport is barely changed, fluctuating around 20 per cent. Although the proportion of civil aviation transport has been very little, but the overall increase trend, from 1990 to 0.1 per cent in 2013 to 0.4 per cent.

As can be seen from Figure 6.2, from the overall trend, CO_2 emissions from traffic and transportation in China increased rapidly from 1990 to 2013, from 120.62 million $MtCO_2$ Eq. in 1990 to 860.54 million $MtCO_2$ Eq. in 2013, with an average annual increase rate of 9.57 per cent, higher than the total annual CO_2 emissions in China of 6.55 per cent growth rate. The proportion of transportation CO_2 emissions to total emissions increased from 4.64 per cent in 1990 to 8.4 per cent in 2013. From this point of view, since 2000, traffic has accelerated the growth of CO_2 emissions, the annual average growth of 11.58 per cent. Compared with the 6.45 per cent average annual growth rate from 1990 to 1999, it is 5.13 percentage points higher.

Figure 6.3 presents the transport structure change in the United States from 1990 to 2011. From the perspective of the structure of transportation, the

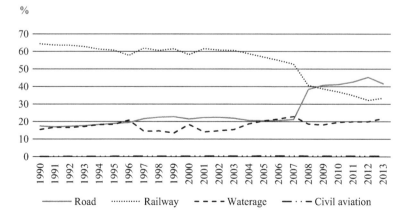

Figure 6.1 The transport structure change in China from 1990 to 2013

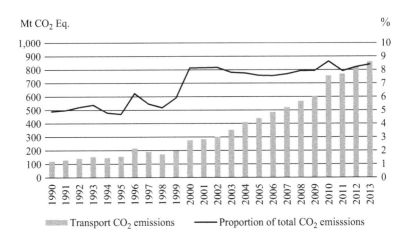

Figure 6.2 The transport CO$_2$ emissions in China from 1990 to 2013

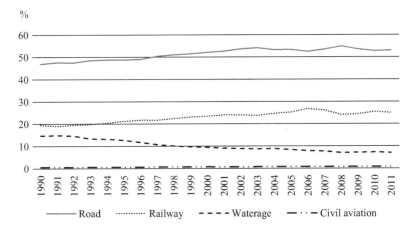

Figure 6.3 The transport structure change in the United States from 1990 to 2011

proportion of all modes of transportation in the United States has not changed too much, and the road-based pattern has always been maintained. From 1990 to 2011, the proportion of highway rose from 46.95 per cent to 52.97 per cent, an increase of 6 percentage points, the proportion of railway increased from 19.48 per cent to 25.04 per cent, an increase of 5.56 per cent. The proportion of waterage transport decreased from 14.67 per cent to 7 per cent, a decrease of 8.67 percentage points. Although the amount of civil aviation turnover increased, its overall size is relatively small, so the change in the amount of turnover did not change, remaining at 0.7 per cent.

The United States, the most industrialized country, has the most CO$_2$ emissions and is much higher than other countries. In Figure 6.4, from 1990 to

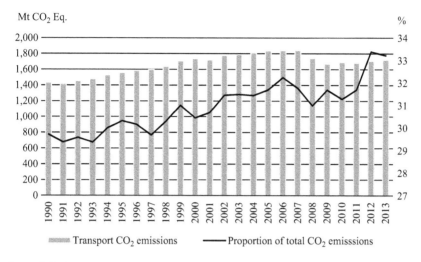

Mt CO$_2$ Eq.

%

▩▩▩ Transport CO$_2$ emissions ——Proportion of total CO$_2$ emisssions

Figure 6.4 The transport CO$_2$ emissions in the United States from 1990 to 2013

2013, US traffic carbon emissions on the overall upward trend with an average annual growth rate of 0.83 per cent from 1433.13 million tons of carbon dioxide equivalent in1990 to 1722.85 million MtCO$_2$ Eq. in 2013. However, from the change stage, the growth rate slowed down significantly, decreased and since 2008 began to decline. Among them, 1990–2000 US traffic carbon emissions showed an average annual growth of 1.94 per cent in 2000–2007, an average annual increase of 1.1 per cent decline. From 2008 onwards, the US carbon emissions decreased by 5.34 per cent in 2009 compared with 2007, down 4.1 per cent compared with 2008, then rebounded slightly. From 2010–2013, the annual average growth rate was 0.77 per cent. From the proportion to total carbon emissions, the proportion of US traffic carbon emissions to total carbon emissions is about 30 per cent, and it shows a slow increase, from 20.71 per cent in 1990 to 33.22 per cent in 2013. In short, compared with the twentieth century, transport carbon emissions growth has reduced significantly in United States since 2000, and traffic carbon emissions growth has been effectively inhibited.

Figure 6.5 shows the structure change in the EU. From 1990 to 2011, the proportion of road, rail, water transport and civil aviation to total turnover in the EU has changed little and has always maintained a road-based pattern. From 1990 to 2011, the proportion of highways increased from 49.54 per cent to 54.32 per cent, an increase of 4.78 per cent; the proportion of railway increased from 22.58 per cent to 19.93 per cent in 2000 and then increased to 21.11 per cent in 2011. Water transport in the EU is second only to the highway: its proportion from 1990 to 2008 did not change significantly, began to decline in 2009, and fell to 22.12 per cent in 2011. Similar to the United States and Japan, the share of civil aviation in the EU is also very small, at 0.6 per cent.

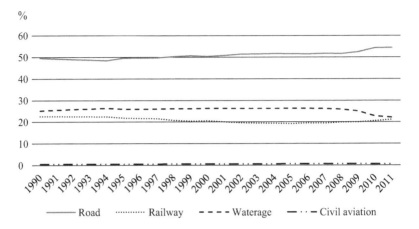

Figure 6.5 The transport structure change in the EU from 1990 to 2011

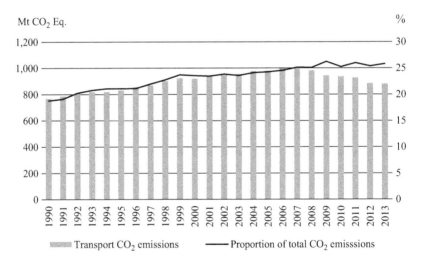

Figure 6.6 The transport CO$_2$ emissions in the EU from 1990 to 2013

With the 2008 financial crisis as a turning point, the EU's carbon emissions also experienced a process of first increase and then decrease. From 1990 to 2007, carbon emissions in transportation increased from 768.23 million MtCO$_2$ Eq. to 1004.71 million MtCO$_2$ Eq., an average annual growth rate of 1.6 per cent. In 2008, carbon emissions from transportation decreased by 24 million MtCO$_2$ Eq. compared to 2007 and then continued to decrease. In 2013, it was 879.59, with an annual reduction rate of 2.18 per cent. But the proportion of EU transport carbon emissions continue to increase, from 20.05 per cent in 1990 to 2013 25.79 per cent.

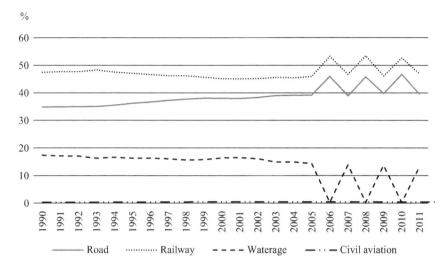

Figure 6.7 The transport structure change in Japan from 1990 to 2011

Japan's transportation structure changed little from 1990 to 2001 (Figure 6.7). From 1990 to 2005, the proportion of railway decreased from 47.44 per cent to 45.94 per cent, but the railway has always been Japan's most important means of transportation. The proportion of road has increased from 34.9 per cent in 1990 to 39.19 per cent in 2005, and the proportion of waterways has decreased from 17.35 per cent in 1990 to 14.4 per cent in 2005. After 2005, the proportion of railway, highway and waterway has fluctuated synchronously. Although the turnover of civil aviation increased continuously, its growth rate was slow: from 1990 to 2011, passenger transport increased from 50,909 million km to 69,692 million people kilometers, and freight turnover increased from 629,754 million tons/km to 93,1044 million tons/km. But its overall size is relatively small, so the amount of turnover in the proportion has not significantly changed, always around 0.4 per cent.

As can be seen in Figure 6.8, the total carbon emissions of Japan has been increasing and decreasing in the past 20 years, from 219.74 million $MtCO_2$ Eq. in 1990 to 273.27 million $MtCO_2$ Eq. in 2001, with an average annual growth rate of 2.02 per cent. Since then, the overall downward trend in 2013, Japan's carbon emissions to 214.93, down 21.35 per cent compared to 2001. The proportion of Japan's traffic carbon emissions first increased and then decreased. The proportion of the total carbon emissions in Japan increased from 20.05 per cent to 23.36 per cent in 1990–1998 and then decreased gradually. Although the year rebounded (22.71 per cent), the downward trend since then has been very obvious: in 2013, the proportion of the total carbon emissions in Japan accounted for 17.29 per cent of carbon emissions. In Japan, rail transportation has become the main mode of transportation, with rail transport including inter-city trains and urban subway and trams.

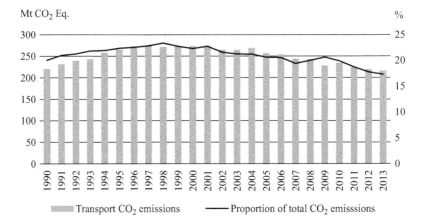

Figure 6.8 The transport CO_2 emissions in Japan from 1990 to 2013

6.3 Data and variables

Through data collection and reorganization, we found that pipe transportation only accounts for a small part in China, the US, EU and Japan. Therefore, this chapter examines the proportion for four transportation methods: highways, railways, waterage (ocean carriage excluded) and civil aviation (international transport excluded), with the independent variables respectively marked as X_1, X_2, X_3 and X_4. CO_2 emissions per unit conversion turnover (1,000kg CO_2 equivalent / 10^7 kg-kilometer) represents the transport pollution degree, which is marked as Y. The passenger-freight conversion coefficients were taken from the report *Energy Consumption, Emissions and Their Comparison among Different Transport Modes*, published by the Integrated Transport Research Center of China Beijing Jiaotong University. The converted passenger transport turnover and the original freight transport turnover were added together to arrive at the total converted turnover.

The passenger and freight transport turnover in data from China, the US, the EU and Japan come from the *China Statistical Yearbook* (2013), *National Transportation Statistics (2013), the Eurostat Yearbook of Energy and Transport (2013), The Automated Vehicle Transport Statistical Yearbook, The Railway Transport Statistical Yearbook, The Civil Aviation Transport Yearbook, and The Inland Vessel Transport Statistical Yearbook (2013)* issued by Japan's Transport Ministry. The CO_2 emissions data came from the World Bank, Carbon Dioxide Information Analysis Center (n.d.).

6.4 Empirical analysis

6.4.1 Parameter stationarity test

The series stationarity test methods were divided into two parts: (1) unit root tests against a common root condition, including a Levin-Lin-Chu test (LLC) test, a Breitung test and a Hadri test, and (2) unit root tests against an individual root condition, including an Im-Pesaran-Shin (IPS) test, a Fisher-ADF test and a Fisher-PP test. The test results showed that the level-series for X_1, X_2, X_3, X_4 and Y were nonstationary, but the first differences series were all stationary (Table 6.1). The stationarity test results for the first difference series are shown in Table 6.1, where the optimal lag intervals were determined using the Schwarz Information Criterion (SIC). This allowed us to perform a panel data cointegration test so as to verify whether there was a long-term, balanced relationship between the transport structure and the per unit CO_2 conversion emissions.

6.4.2 Panel data cointegration test

The panel data cointegration test had two divisions: one based on the Engle and Granger two-step method, with the applicable test methods being the Pedroni test and the Kao test, and the other based on the Johansen cointegration test. The null hypothesis for this was that there was no cointegration relationship between the panel data. The results of the cointegration test aimed at the first difference series of X_1, X_2, X_3, X_4 and Y are shown in Tables 6.2 and 6.3, wherein the lag intervals for the Kao test and the Pedroni test were determined

Table 6.1 The parameter stationarity test for the first order difference sequences

Variables	ΔX_1	ΔX_2	ΔX_3	ΔX_4	ΔY
LLC	−15.582(0.00)*	−11.41(0.00)*	−12.95(0.00)*	−3.311(0.00)*	−15.29(0.00)*
Breitung	−3.474(0.00)*	1.668(0.95)	−2.882(0.00)*	−2.052(0.02)*	−4.404(0.00)*
Hadri	0.943(0.172)*	1.14(0.127)*	1.404(0.08)*	5.2757(0.00)	2.781(0.0027)
IPS	−13.306(0.00)*	−9.409(0.00)*	−12.99(0.00)*	−3.559(0.00)*	−12.11(0.00)*
Fisher-ADF	249.67(0.00)*	100.01(0.00)*	175.94(0.00)*	26.243(0.00)*	131.68(0.00)*
Fisher-PP	303.93(0.00)*	122.23(0.00)*	232.46(0.00)*	56.646(0.00)*	325.80(0.00)*
Stability judgement	stable	stable	stable	stable	stable

Note: *signifies that, when the significance level was under 5 per cent, we rejected the null hypothesis and accepted the alternative hypothesis.

Table 6.2 Kao and Pedroni panel cointegration test

Test methods	Test hypothesis	Statistical name	Statistic (P-Value)
Kao test	H_0 : no cointegration relationship ($\rho = 1$)	ADF	−5.6473(0.0000)*
Pedroni test	$H_0:\rho_i = 1\ H_i : \rho_i < 1$	Panel v-Statistic	−0.7895(0.7851)
		Panel rho-Statistic	0.1949(0.5773)
		Panel PP-Statistic	−2.1361(0.0163)*
		Panel ADF Statistic	−2.2194(0.0132)*
	$H_0:\rho_i = 1\ H_i : \rho_i < 1$	Group-rho-Statistic	0.6772(0.7809)
		Group PP-Statistic	−3.7389(0.0001)*
		Group ADF Statistic	−3.1665(0.0008)*

Note: *denotes that test result rejected the null hypothesis and accepted the alternative hypothesis under the significance level of 5 per cent.

Table 6.3 Johansen panel cointegration test

Null hypothesis	Fisher stat (from trace test) (P-Value)	Fisher stat (from λ-max test) (P-Value)
No cointegration vector	59.99 (0.0000)*	526.8 (0.0000)*
At most 1	89.49 (0.0000)*	100.5 (00000)*
At most 2	37.77 (0.0000)*	19.96 (0.0005)*
At most 3	22.03 (0.0002)*	20.23 (0.0004)*
At most 4	6.641 (0.1561)	6.589 (0.1593)

Note: *denotes that test result rejected the null hypothesis and accepted the alternative hypothesis under the significance level of 5 per cent.

using the SIC principle. The Johansen panel cointegration test selected such cases as the series has a determinacy trend, and the cointegration equation only has an intercept.

Tables 6.2 and 6.3 indicate that a cointegration relationship exists between the first difference series for the transport structure and the per unit converted turnover carbon emissions. The result of the Johansen panel cointegration test indicated that there were four cointegration vectors in the panel data.

6.4.3 Model estimation

Before the model estimation, it is necessary to introduce a classification for the panel data model, including variable interception model and the variable coefficient model. Further, the variable interception model and the variable coefficient model include a fixed effect variable intercept model, a random effect variable intercept model, a fixed effect variable coefficient model and a random effect variable coefficient model. The fixed effect model uses constant terms to reflect the effects of the variable, which is ignored but reflects the individual differences in the cross section. The inception in the random effect model includes both constant terms and random terms, with the latter expressing the effect of the variable which is ignored but reflects the cross sectional difference.

Hausman test

When building the panel data model, first, it is necessary to determine whether to build a fixed effect model or a random effect model. Hausman (1978) developed a strict method, which is called the Hausman test. The null hypothesis is that, in the random effect model, the individual effect is irrelevant to the explanatory variables. Specifically, we will first establish the random effect model and then verify whether this model satisfies the null hypothesis. If so, we will then build the random effect model. If not, a fixed effect model will be built.

Here, we performed the Hausman test to identify the first differences for X_1, X_2, X_3, X_4 and Y. The statistical value for $W = 4.272$, $P = 0.0866 > 0.05$. The null hypothesis was rejected. Therefore, we will build a fixed effect model.

Model building

The general form for the panel data model is presented in Equation 6.1.

$$y_{it} = \alpha_i + x_{it}\beta_i + \mu_{it}, \quad i = 1, \cdots, n, \quad t = 1, \cdots T$$

$$i = 1, \cdots, n \tag{6.1}$$

Where $x_{it} = 1 \times k$ vector, $\beta_i = k \times 1$ vector, k is the number of explanatory variables, n is the number of cross sectional individuals, and T is the time series length. In this chapter, the number of cross sections $n = 4$, the number of explanatory variables $k = 4$ and the time series length $T = 21$. Equation 6.1 has three popular conditions:

Condition 1: $\alpha_i = \alpha_j$, $\beta_i = \beta_j$
Condition 2: $\alpha_i \neq \alpha_j$, $\beta_i = \beta_j$
Condition 3: $\alpha_i \neq \alpha_j$, $\beta_i \neq \beta_j$

Condition 1 is a fixed parameter model, without any individual effect or structure change at the cross section. Conditions 2 and 3 are, respectively, a variable interception model and a variable coefficient model. The key to constructing the panel data model is to determine the model's form. A widely used test for this is a covariance analysis, namely the F test. The main task is to test two hypotheses, as illustrated in Tables 6.2 and 6.3.

Hypothesis 1: The gradient is the same at different cross sectional sample points and time points but different at the interceptions (Equation 6.2).

$$H_1 : y_{it} = \alpha_i + x_{it}\beta + \mu_{it} \tag{6.2}$$

Hypothesis 2: The intercept and the gradient are different in the cross section samples and at the time points (Equation 6.3).

$$H_2 : y_{it} = \alpha + x_{it}\beta + \mu_{it} \tag{6.3}$$

Decision rules: if H_2 is accepted, a fixed parameter model is built (Condition 1), and the test ends. If H_2 is rejected, then H_1 is tested. If H_1 is accepted, the model is a variable inception model (Condition 2). If H_1 is rejected, the model is a variable coefficient model (Condition 3). According to the Hausman test, the model should be set as a fixed effect. Thus, the steps for the F test in the chapter should be as follows:

1   Construct the variable coefficient fixed effect model, and determine the residual sum of squares $S_1 = 0.07977$ and the degree of freedom $n(T - k - 1) = 64$.
2   Construct the variable intercept fixed effect model, and determine the residual sum of squares $S_2 = 0.1962$ and the degree of freedom $(n - 1) k = 12$.

3   Construct the fixed parameter model, and determine the residual Sum of Squares S_3 = 0.2020 and the degree of freedom $(n - 1)(k + 1)$ = 15.

Test the F statistic for H_2 using Equation 6.4.

$$F_2 = \frac{(S_3 - S_1) / [(n - 1)(k + 1)]}{S_1 / [n(T - k - 1)]} \tag{6.4}$$

After referring to the F test distribution table, we determine the critical value for the statistic F_2 $F[(n - 1)(k + 1)\ n(T - k - 1)]$ = $F(15, 64)$ = 1.83, 6.5369 >1.83, so hypothesis H_2 is rejected. Continue the test for hypothesis H_1. The F statistic for H_1 can be found through Equation 6.5.

$$F_1 = \frac{(S_2 - S_1) / [(n - 1)k]}{S_1 / [n(T - k - 1)]} = 7.7826 \tag{6.5}$$

After referring to the F test distribution table, we determine the critical value for statistic F_1 $F[(n - 1)\ k,\ n(T - k - 1)]$ = $F(12, 64)$ = 1.91, 7.7826 > 1.91. Therefore, hypothesis H_1 is rejected, which indicates that we should build a fixed effect coefficient model. This chapter used Eviews 7.2 software to establish the fixed effect variable coefficient model for the first difference series for X_1, X_2, X_3, X_4 and Y, as shown in Equation 6.6.

$$\Delta Y_i = \begin{matrix} \alpha_i \\ \begin{bmatrix} 0.0256 \\ -0.0131 \\ -0.0009 \\ -0.0116 \end{bmatrix} \end{matrix} + \begin{matrix} \beta_{1i} \\ \begin{bmatrix} -1.7656 \\ 4.4391 \\ 2.4570 \\ 3.4729 \end{bmatrix} \end{matrix} \Delta X_1 + \begin{matrix} \beta_{2i} \\ \begin{bmatrix} -0.3802 \\ -2.6056 \\ -2.2145 \\ -3.6283 \end{bmatrix} \end{matrix} \Delta X_2$$

$$+ \begin{matrix} \beta_{3i} \\ \begin{bmatrix} -0.0556 \\ 0.8046 \\ -22.1045 \\ -0.0933 \end{bmatrix} \end{matrix} \Delta X_3 + \begin{matrix} \beta_{4i} \\ \begin{bmatrix} 54.5336 \\ 54.9905 \\ -27.0647 \\ 149.6716 \end{bmatrix} \end{matrix} \Delta X_4 \tag{6.6}$$

In Equation 6.6, i = 1, 2, 3, 4, is the cross section sample point. The estimators stand for China, the US, the EU and Japan respectively from the top down in the matrix. The significance of each explanatory variable for Equation 6.6 is listed in Table 6.4.

Table 6.4 shows that most estimators passed the T-test. The determination coefficient for the model is R^2 = 0.8859, and the corrected determination coefficient is 0.8520. This indicates that the model achieved a good fit, which could well explain the impact of the transport structure on CO_2 emissions per unit of converted turnover.

Table 6.4 Significance test for the fixed effect variable coefficient regression model

Variables	ΔX_1	ΔX_2	ΔX_3	ΔX_4
China	−3.0696 (0.0031)	−0.7374(0.4636)	−0.3725 (0.7108)	−0.866 (0.3897)
US	0.3248 (0.7464)	2.093 (0.0403)	0.393 (0.6952)	2.455 (0.0168)
EU	−2.6041 (0.0114)	−2.76 (0.0075)	−2.70 (0.0087)	−0.69 (0.4923)
Japan	3.1538 (0.0025)	0.56 (0.5720)	0.319 (0.7507)	2.768 (0.0074)

6.5 Results and discussion

From the estimated results from Equation 6.6, we analyzed the impact of the different transport structures on the CO_2 emissions per unit of converted turnover in China, the US, the EU and Japan.

1   First, we analyzed the coefficient vector β_{1i}. A positive coefficient indicates that an increase in the percentage of highway turnover X_1 would lead to an increase in per unit of converted turnover carbon emissions Y. From Equation 6.6, we can see that a *1 per cent increase in the* highway percentage would cause a **4.4391** per cent, **2.4570** per cent and **3.4729** per cent *drop in* per unit CO_2 conversion turnover emissions in the US, the EU and Japan respectively. As disclosed in the report, *Study of Transport Energy Consumption and Carbon Emissions* (Shi, 2011), highway transport accounts for up to 90 per cent of passenger transport carbon emissions and up to 25–30 per cent of freight transport carbon emissions, forming the main CO_2 resource from 1990–2008. As seen in Equation 6.6, transport carbon emissions in China have an inverse relation with the highway percentage, as the Ministry of Transport and the National Statistic Administration of China changed the highway statistics method in 2008, meaning that the highway freight transport statistical data increased significantly after 2008. At the same time, technical progress and other factors led to a decrease in CO_2 emissions per unit of converted turnover. Therefore, it is not strange that there is a negative coefficient in Equation 6.6.

2   The coefficient β_{2i} indicates the change in the carbon emissions per unit of converted turnover caused by a percentage change in railway turnover. From Equation 6.6, it can be seen that the coefficients are all negative, which indicates that an increase in the railway percentage in China, the US, the EU and Japan leads to a CO_2 reduction. In comparison, the impact is most significant in Japan (−3.6283), which is because the Japanese government pays significant attention to optimizing the transport structure so as to reduce emissions. The coefficient for China is only −0.3802, which may be the result of the rapid development in highway transport in recent years, bringing about an increase in the highway share but a decrease in the railway share. From 1990 to 2013, the percentage of highway transport increased from 17 per cent to 45 per cent. At the same time, that of railway transport decreased from 0.65 to 0.32. Such a reverse turn weakened the effect of railway transport on transport carbon emissions.

3   The coefficient β_{3i} signifies that the carbon emissions have a negative relation-
    ship with the waterage percentage. In comparison, the change in the waterway
    percentage in the EU would greatly promote a reduction in carbon emissions.
    A 1 per cent increase in the waterway share would lead to a decrease of 22.11
    per cent in CO_2 emissions in the transportation industry. The reason is that
    many EU members border on the Mediterranean and the Baltic, so rely greatly
    on marine transport for trade. The data shows that the marine percentage in
    the EU accounted for over 35 per cent from 1995 to 2008, which was just
    behind that of highway transport (40–45 per cent). In contrast, a percent-
    age increment in water transport in the US has a positive relationship with
    the CO_2 emissions per unit of converted turnover because, in this period, the
    railway transport percentage in the US increased significantly (19.48 per cent
    up to 25.04 per cent). This clean transport makes a great contribution to car-
    bon emissions reduction. At the same time, the percentage of water transport
    decreased from 14.67 per cent to 6.99 per cent, which means that the percent-
    age of water transport has a positive relationship with carbon emissions.

4   Because civil aviation has the highest carbon emissions, the coefficient β_{4i} is
    obviously larger than β_{1i}, β_{2i} or β_{3i}. As this transport sector has very high car-
    bon emissions, only a small increase in the civil aviation percentage could lead
    to much larger increases in carbon emissions. In 2008, the carbon emissions in
    the United States civil aviation sector were 1750 kg CO_2 equivalent $/10^7$ kg-
    kilometer, while in Japan it was 14.39, which is significantly higher than high-
    ways (2.37), railways (0.22) and water transport (0.395). In the model, only
    in the EU does the civil aviation percentage have a negative relationship with
    the carbon emissions performance at roughly –27.07 per cent. On the one
    hand, this carbon emissions performance is significantly lower than that in the
    US, China and Japan. The EU's average carbon emissions performance (CO_2
    emissions per unit of converted turnover) in the civil aviation sector was only
    425 kg CO_2 equivalent $/10^7$ kg-kilometer from 1995 to 2008. In addition,
    there was a year-on-year decreasing trend. On the other hand, from 1990 to
    2011, the mean percentage for civil aviation was a poor 0.59 per cent, a share
    of 2.3 per cent for carbon emissions sources. Under the comprehensive action
    of both factors, there is an inverse relationship between the EU's civil aviation
    percentage and the carbon emissions performance in Equation 6.6.

6.6 Conclusions

The empirical results showed that an increase in railway and waterage percentages would be helpful for carbon emissions reduction, but the degree of influence differed between the four countries. Therefore, China can be inspired to
improve its transportation structure in several ways: for passenger transportation,
we should learn from Japan (as described earlier, Japan's railway use contributes
greatly to carbon emissions reductions) and develop subways in large cities as well
as increasing the railway share between cities. At the same time, certain policies
should be introduced to restrict the use of cars.

7 Conclusion and future work

7.1 Research conclusion

The *Strategic Action Plan for Energy Development (2014–2020)*, published by the Office of State Council shows that implementing a "green transportation" plan is an important act in promoting an energy consumption revolution: within the plan, technologies to improve transportation resource efficiency, the construction of transportation infrastructure and the modification of transportation structures are the main breakthrough directions. The Ministry of Transportation also published *Opinions on Accelerating the Application of New Energy Vehicles (Draft)* (*Draft* for short); the *Draft* mentioned that up to the year 2020, the ratio of new-energy resource vehicles in areas such as public transportation, taxi service and delivery services must not be lower than 30 per cent. In the United States, some electric public transportation vehicles have already been put to use; according to statistics provided by the American Public Transportation Association (www.apta.com), in 2005, electric busses only made up 1 per cent of the market share, in 2014, this number has increased to 17 per cent. In early 2015, research from the World Resources Institute (WRI, https://www.wri.org/) shows that the United States has been advancing towards "green transportation"; market data also shows, in the past 5 years, the number of SUVs with a fuel efficiency of 25 mpg or higher has doubled and the number of cars with a fuel efficiency of 40 mpg or higher has increased 7 times in the past 5 years. Using the greenhouse gas and fuel economy standard recently released by the Environmental Protection Agency (EPA) and the Department of Transportation (DOT), in 2025, cars and pick-up trucks' fuel consumption will only be half of that of a current new vehicle. Since the emissions of passenger cars and pick-up trucks accounted for 16.5 per cent of US greenhouse gas emissions, therefore, a cleaner transportation system is also good news for the Earth. Studies show that new policies can broaden the use of high-efficiency transportation tools, lower carbon emissions and save more money for consumers. Innovation and the development of transportation energy saving technologies, adjustment of the transportation structure and support for the transportation energy saving and emissions reduction policies are the main breakthrough directions for future global transportation energy saving and emissions reduction.

The research on the problem of transportation energy saving and emissions reduction, under the frequent smog weather circumstances, has become a scientific problem with important practical value and urgent need for theory. In 2014, Beijing's PM2.5 source analysis research shows that motor vehicles consisted of 31.1 per cent of the total PM2.5 pollution contribution sources in Beijing in that year. Moreover, motor vehicles also make a comprehensive contribution to the production of PM2.5 pollution emissions. Other than directly emitting PM2.5, gas pollutants produced by motor vehicles are not only the "primary resource" of secondary particles and nitrate in PM2.5, but also an important "catalyst" in the increasing oxidation of the atmosphere. Moreover, motor vehicles also act as a "mixer" for the emitted dust on the road. Not long after, the report released by Shanghai Environment Monitoring Center also displayed a graph showing the PM2.5 sources in Shanghai, amongst all, the "contribution" from the transportation industry accounted for 31 per cent. In recent years, as China's transportation infrastructure improves significantly, the freight and turnover volume continues to increase, and the transportation industry continues to develop at a rapid pace. Currently, China's public transportation consists mainly of roads and railways, which accounted for 48.21 per cent and 33.93 per cent of the public transportation turnover volume in 2013 respectively. The rapid development of the transportation industry will be accompanied by the rapid increase of transportation energy consumption. According to the China transportation energy source statistics caliber, transportation energy consumption in China has increased 10.33 per cent annually between 1990 and 2012. This is 3 times the average increase rate of the entire country (3.74 per cent); it is the industry with the fastest energy consumption increase in China for the past 20 years. According to statistics from the World Bank, Carbon Dioxide Information Analysis Center (n.d.), CO_2 emissions in China's transportation area has increased from 108.66 million tons in 1990 to 623.32 million tons in 2011, growing 9.19 per cent annually. China's leading carbon emissions in the transportation area is mainly concentrated on the roads: in 2011, 78.93 per cent of carbon emissions were produced on the road. Therefore, promoting energy saving and emissions reduction in the transportation structure is the key problem as China currently develops environmentally friendly transportation.

Since transportation is the lifeline of a country's economic and social development, more and more researchers are starting to focus on the transportation problem. Amongst all, the energy consumption and carbon emissions problem has naturally become a hot research topic. Previous research made detailed analyses of the transportation energy consumption structure, energy consumption level calculation, a low-carbon evaluation index and plans to develop low-carbon transportation. From an energy saving and emissions reduction perspective, in order to achieve the goal of energy saving and being environmentally friendly through technological improvement, transportation structure and policy, a complete analysis of factors that affect transportation energy consumption is required. Under the premise of considering all other factors, calculating energy consumption of different transportation methods will provide a reasonable proof for the adjustment plan of the transportation structure.

Based on this, this chapter will first analyze factors affecting the transportation needs. This is very meaningful for easing air pollution caused by current transportation. By establishing a structural formula model and using a Bayesian estimation method, this chapter compares the effect of potential factors such as transportation infrastructure, transportation cost, and economic activity on the need for road transportation in China and the United States. The results show that, in the analysis of factors affecting the need for road transportation, China and United States behaved similarly in the following way: economic activity had the biggest direct effect, followed by transportation infrastructure, and transportation cost had the smallest direct effect. After considering the indirect effect caused by interaction between all potential factors, transportation infrastructure had the biggest overall impact, followed by economic activity, and transportation cost still had the smallest direct effect. In the analysis of potential factors affecting the need for road transportation in China and the United States, two countries behaved differently in the following way: the effect of transportation cost on the need for road transportation in the United States is much smaller than that of China, and Chinese consumers are more sensitive to transportation cost compared to American consumers. This is mainly because transportation and fuel costs still remain at a relatively high level compared to the average Chinese income.

Secondly, after considering the demonstration effect of other countries' transportation development on China's transportation energy saving and emissions reduction, and the accessibility of data, this chapter selected passenger turnover volume and transportation carbon emissions data consisting of four transportation methods (road, railway, water, commercial airline) in China, The United States, European Union and Japan between 1990–2011 and then constructed a fixed effect variable coefficient model. The analysis shows that increasing the ratio of water transportation and railway transportation will decrease transportation carbon emissions. A 1 per cent increase Japan's railway transportation resulted in a 3.63 per cent decrease in its carbon emissions; a 1 per cent increase in the EU's water transportation resulted in a 22.11 per cent decrease in its carbon emissions, putting them in first place in these two types of transportation structural emissions respectively. In China, the numbers are 0.38 per cent and 0.06 per cent respectively. This chapter will not only expand research for transportation structural energy saving emissions reduction from a theoretical analysis to a quantitative calculation; it will also provide a reference for optimization of China's transportation structure through a parallel analysis between different countries. The results show that there exists a long-term equilibrium relationship between transportation structure and carbon emissions performance and that optimizing the transportation structure is a critical step in the current transportation energy saving and emissions reduction.

Moreover, air pollution caused by oil product consumption in the transportation area has become an important source for smog component in cities and regions of China. Price can be the main means of adjusting the supply and demand, but it has asymmetric characteristics. Analyzing the asymmetrical effect on transportation need caused by the change in the crude oil price has practical significance. Based on this, after breaking down the gas and diesel prices in China, Japan and the United States, this chapter will discuss the asymmetrical effects of these prices on the passenger and commercial demand of each country. The analysis result shows that, currently, the relatively high oil prices have not caused a decrease in China's transportation demand; however, in the United and Japan, there exists a negative relationship between transportation need and prices. The change in oil price has not had a significant impact on the Japanese transportation. The effect of asymmetric change in oil price on the transportation demand in China and the United States both showed a significant impact during the price recovery period. Meanwhile, commercial transportation needs react more sensitively to changes in oil prices than do passenger transportation needs in both countries.

Finally, since China's current main methods of transportation are railway, road, air, water, pipe etc. Amongst all, the transportation energy consumption in the railway area has produced a detailed result (a series of reports written by Professor Fu Zhihuan of the Chinese Academy of Engineering and his team), transportation energy consumption in road and aviation areas lack research, water and pipe transportation has a small effect because they account for a small ratio. Based on this, this chapter will use aviation and road as examples and analyze China's fuel consumption in air transportation and energy consumption in road transportation. First, the fast development of China's economic society has caused a continuous increase in its aviation transportation needs, and this is accompanied by a significant increase in aviation fuel consumption. Increases in the oil prices and the need for emissions reduction have caused the cost of fuel to increase significantly in the aviation industry. Therefore, controlling the overly rapid growth of aviation fuel consumption has become a realistic need for airlines in order to control costs and realize continuous development. However, the premise is to conduct reasonable analysis and predictions on aviation fuel consumption. Based on this, this chapter will break down the need for aviation fuel into two factors – efficiency (aviation fuel efficiency) and total volume (aviation transportation total turnover volume) – then use path analysis technology to choose the core factors affecting the two indices. After choosing the model, it will conduct an analysis and formulate predictions on aviation fuel efficiency and aviation transportation total turnover volume from two dimensions – single variable (ETS and ARIMA models) and multivariable (Bayesian multivariable regression). Finally, this chapter will compute the two results to analyze and formulate predictions on the consumption need for aviation fuel. The results show that every 1 per cent increase in the airline carrying rate will result in a 0.8 per cent increase in aviation fuel efficiency, every 1 per cent increase in the urbanization rate will result in a 3.8 per cent increase in the aviation transportation total turnover volume and every 1 per cent increase in the GDP per capita will result in a 0.4 per cent increase in the aviation transportation total turnover volume. Towards the end of the 12th Five-Year Plan, fuel consumption in Chinese aviation will increase to nearly 28 million tons. In 2020, fuel consumption in Chinese aviation will increase to nearly

50 million tons. Moreover, as China's industrialization and urbanization pace increases, transportation needs increase as well. Since energy consumption and pollution in China's transportation industry account for a significant percentage and is increasing at a rapid pace, therefore, it is a key area in China's energy saving and emissions reduction. This chapter first comparatively analyzes the road turn-over volume and GDP's historical trend charts of economic bodies such as the United States, Japan, the European Union, China etc. The analysis showed the two subjects have a clear "Inverted L" shape, then this chapter further explored the potential relationship between the total turnover volume, GDP and road energy consumption. Second, this chapter used path analysis model and analyzed every variable's effect mechanism on road energy consumption from multiple perspective such as demand, supply, cost and country policies etc. Results from the elastic analysis shows: when all other factors remain unchanged, every 1 per cent in GDP resulted in a 0.58 per cent increase in the need for road energy con-sumption; every 1 per cent increase in the road transportation total turnover vol-ume resulted in a 0.34 per cent increase in road energy consumption; every 1 per cent increase in the total road kilometer count resulted in a 0.9 per cent increase in road energy consumption; every 1 per cent increase in the urbanization rate resulted in a 2.83 per cent increase in road energy consumption. Afterwards, this chapter selected the core affecting factors using the Bayesian model average method. Finally, on the basis of model selection, it conducted analysis and pre-dictions for the road energy consumption from two perspectives – single variable (ETS and ARIMA models) and multivariable (scenario analysis). The prediction result shows that every 1 per cent increase will result in a 0.33 per cent increase in the need for road energy consumption and that every 1 per cent increase in urbanization rate will result in a 1.26 per cent increase in road energy consump-tion. Nearing the end of the 12th Five-Year Plan, road energy consumption in China will increase to nearly 226 million tons. In 2021, it will increase to nearly 379 million tons.

There are many advanced foreign methods to decrease transportation pollu-tion emissions that China learn from; however, since China is under the special circumstance of not wanting to sacrifice economic development, therefore, con-sidering transportation energy saving and emissions reduction under the need for economic development, energy resource, cost, technology and environment regulations needs to be further explored and researched.

7.2 Questions for further research

This chapter mainly used Bayesian statistics and decision theory and structural model, macroeconomics model and econometric model theory to conduct a complete and detailed analysis of the current and future state of China's transpor-tation energy consumption, China and foreign countries' transportation energy consumption, core factors/variables affecting transportation energy consump-tion and the energy consumption of different transportation methods from two different perspectives – single variable and multivariable. This analysis concluded some research results and innovative theories. However, in order to have more practical application, future work can be improved in several ways.

One way is through transportation energy saving and emissions reduction through multi-target demand, control research and optimization of the transportation system. The evolution of the transportation industry is organically connected to the socio-economic development process; there exists a complicated two-way mechanism between the two subjects. This mechanism is different in practice due to differences in environment and time. At the same time, it also directly affects the evolution of transportation structure, technological improvement and management abilities. All these factors will also affect energy saving and emissions reduction in the transportation industry. Looking at China's current state, economic development needs the support of continuously growing transportation volume. Transportation energy saving and emissions reduction must be realized through the transportation structural adjustment and technological advancement. China must reference international development and evolution patterns; research the evolution of the Chinese transportation industry and the dynamic two-way mechanism of socio-economic development process; analyze China's current transportation energy saving and emissions reduction state and affecting factors and development trends; and provide an energy saving and emissions reduction realization path that satisfies society's economic needs through structural adjustment and technological development.

The analysis of the effect of transportation energy saving and emissions reduction in China under the guidance of the market-oriented economic policy and its synergy. Currently, China's economic development has placed a continuously growing need on the total transportation volume. But the interaction of different methods of transportation is significant, and the energy consumption difference between the methods is significant. Using the market economy to change transportation structure, to improve transportation fuel economy, to improve transportation efficiency, to reduce pollution intensity is a long-term sustainable development model for China. Therefore, it must prioritize public transportation to promote "easing traffic and reducing emissions" in cities. Research must examine appropriate public transportation prices (using the dynamic pricing theory in profit management) and tax issues; must calculate and analyze the effects, mechanisms and paths of different economic policies and policy combinations (different tax policies such as including transportation price and its structure, fuel tax and consumption tax etc.); and must utilize economic policy to adjust transportation demand in order to develop appropriate, market-oriented transportation economic policies. Therefore, analyzing the effect of changing market-oriented economic means on transportation energy consumption and transportation pollution emissions has significant practical value and theory demand for transportation structure and is a scientific problem that needs to be solved.

Another task for future research is through the simulation and analysis of demand-side management in transportation for urban and regional transportation energy saving and emissions reduction. Transportation is the engine of economic development, and the 18th CPC National Congress decided that urbanization is the new engine of China's economic society development. However, the frequent "smog" and the great number of "traffic jam cities" have hindered the development of urbanization. Therefore, city and regional transportation energy saving and emissions reduction problem has become a scientific problem with significant practical value and great urgency. Referencing advanced foreign methods and analyzing China's transportation system in depth can produce potential analysis, and a path to, solving transportation energy saving and emissions reduction using market means. However, at the city and regional level, the special characteristics of particular cities and regions must be considered, and theoretical models must be adjusted in order to guide economic decision-making, to help China solve the "smog" problem and to provide theoretical proof and policy reference for realizing sustainable construction and development. This is the ultimate scientific problem that needs to be solved.

References

Al-Ghandoor, A., Jaber, J., Al-Hinti, I., and Abdallat, Y. (2013). Statistical assessment and analyses of the determinants of transportation sector gasoline demand in Jordan. *Transportation Research Part A: Policy and Practice, 50*, 129–138.

Allan, G., Hanley, N., McGregor, P., Swales, K., and Turner, K. (2007). The impact of increased efficiency in the industrial use of energy: A computable general equilibrium analysis for the United Kingdom. *Energy Economics, 29*(4), 779–798.

Anable, J., Brand, C., Tran, M., and Eyre, N. (2012). Modelling transport energy demand: A socio-technical approach. *Energy Policy, 41*, 125–138.

Andrawis, R. R., Atiya, A. F., and El-Shishiny, H. (2011). Combination of long term and short term forecasts, with application to tourism demand forecasting. *International Journal of Forecasting, 27*(3), 870–886.

Atack, J., Bateman, F., Haines, M., and Margo, R. A. (2010). Did railroads induce or follow economic growth? *Social Science History, 34*(2), 171–197.

Babikian, R., Lukachko, S. P., and Waitz, I. A. (2002). The historical fuel efficiency characteristics of regional aircraft from technological, operational, and cost perspectives. *Journal of Air Transport Management, 8*(6), 389–400.

Baghestani, H. (2010). Forecasting the 10-year US treasury rate. *Journal of Forecasting, 29*(8), 673–688.

Bates, J. M., and Granger, C. W. (1969). The combination of forecasts. *Journal of the Operational Research Society, 20*(4), 451–468.

Bernstein, G. W. (2002). Aviation demand forecasting: A survey of methodologies. *Transportation Research Board Report, 7*(12), 134–149.

Bianchi, L., Jarrett, J., and Hanumara, R. C. (1998). Improving forecasting for telemarketing centers by ARIMA modeling with intervention. *International Journal of Forecasting, 14*(4), 497–504.

Boshoff, W. H. (2010). Petrol, diesel fuel and jet fuel demand in South Africa: 1998–2009. Available at SSRN: http://ssrn.com/abstract=1661021 or http://dx.doi.org/10.2139/ssrn.1661021

Boutahar, M. (2007). Optimal prediction with nonstationary ARFIMA model. *Journal of Forecasting, 26*(2), 95–111.

Butler, N. A. (1999). Updating the forecast function of ARIMA models and the link with DLMs. *Journal of Forecasting, 18*(4), 275–284.

Bresson, E., Chevassut, O., Essiari, A., and Pointcheval, D. (2004). Mutual authentication and group key agreement for low-power mobile devices. *Computer Communications, 27*(17), 1730–1737.

CEIC Database (n.d.). Available at: http://cn.ceibs.edu/library-database

Chai, J., Guo, J. E., Meng, L., and Wang, S. Y. (2011). Exploring the core factors and its dynamic effects on oil price: an application on path analysis and BVAR-TVP model. *Energy Policy*, *39*(12), 8022–8036.

Chai, J., Guo, J. E., Wang, S. Y., and Lai, K. K. (2009). Why does energy intensity fluctuate in China?. *Energy Policy*, *37*(12), 5717–5731.

Chang, S. Y., Hu, X. J., Ou, X. M., and Zhang, X. L. (2010). Decomposition analysis of intercity passenger transportation energy consumption in China Population. *Resources and Environment*, *3*, 24–29.

Chatfield, C. (1988). What is the 'best' method of forecasting? *Journal of Applied Statistics*, *15*(1), 19–38.

Chatfield, C. (1996). Model uncertainty and forecast accuracy. *Journal of Forecasting*, *15*(7), 495–508.

Chen, Y. C., and Fan, Y. Y. (2014). Coping with technology uncertainty in transportation fuel portfolio design. *Transportation Research Part D: Transport and Environment*, *32*, 354–361.

Chèze, B., Gastineau, P., and Chevallier, J. (2011). Forecasting world and regional aviation jet fuel demands to the mid-term (2025). *Energy Policy*, *39*(9), 5147–5158.

Chi, J., and Baek, J. (2012). Price and income elasticities of demand for air transportation: Empirical evidence from US airfreight industry. *Journal of Air Transport Management*, *20*, 18–19.

China National Bureau of Statistics (n.d.) *China Statistical Yearbook*. Beijing: China Statistics Press.

China National Bureau of Statistics, *China Statistical Yearbook[M]*. Beijing: China Statistics Press, 2014.

Cholette, P. A. (1982). Prior information and ARIMA forecasting. *Journal of Forecasting*, *1*(4), 375–383.

Chunark, P., Promjiraprawat, K., and Limmeechokchai, B. (2014). Impacts of reduction target and taxation on Thailand's power system planning towards 2030. *Energy Procedia*, *52*, 82–92.

Cohen-Blankshtain, G. (2008). Framing transport – environmental policy: The case of company car taxation in Israel. *Transportation Research Part D: Transport and Environment*, *13*, 65–74.

Cui, Q., and Li, Y. (2014). The evaluation of transportation energy efficiency: An application of three-stage virtual frontier DEA. *Transportation Research Part D: Transport and Environment*, *29*, 1–11.

Dargay, J., and Gately, D. (1997). The demand for transportation fuels: Imperfect price-reversibility? *Transportation Research Part B: Methodological*, *31*(1), 71–82.

De Gooijer, J. G., and Hyndman, R. J. (2006). 25 years of time series forecasting. *International Journal of Forecasting*, *22*(3), 443–473.

Fan, L. J., and Qin, Q. L. (2013). The optimization model and empirical analysis for vehicle routing problems of s-company with time windows based on C-W algorithm. *Journal of System and Management Sciences*, *2*, 20–28.

Fildes, R. (1983). An evaluation of Bayesian forecasting. *Journal of Forecasting*, *2*(2), 137–150.

Fu, M., and Kelly, J. A. (2012). Carbon related taxation policies for road transport: Efficacy of ownership and usage taxes, and the role of public transport and motorist cost perception on policy outcomes. *Transport Policy*, *22*, 57–69.

Fukuda, K. (2009). Related-variables selection in temporal disaggregation. *Journal of Forecasting*, *28*(4), 343–357.

Gately, D. (1992). Imperfect price-reversibility of US gasoline demand: Asymmetric responses to price increases and declines. *The Energy Journal, 13*(4), 179–207.

Gelper, S., Fried, R., and Croux, C. (2010). Robust forecasting with exponential and Holt – Winters smoothing. *Journal of Forecasting, 29*(3), 285–300.

Godsill, S. J. (2001). On the relationship between Markov chain Monte Carlo methods for model uncertainty. *Journal of Computational and Graphical Statistics, 10*(2), 230–248.

Goodwin, P. B. (1995). *Empirical evidence on induced traffic: A review and synthesis.* Oxford: University of Oxford, Transport Studies Unit.

Goodwin, P. B., Dargay, J., and Hanly, M. (2004). Elasticities of road traffic and fuel consumption with respect to price and income: A review. *Transport Reviews, 24*(3), 275–292.

Graham, D. J., and Glaister, S. (2004). Road traffic demand elasticity estimates: a review. *Transport Reviews, 24*(3), 261–274.

Green, P. J. (1995). Reversible jump Markov chain Monte Carlo computation and Bayesian model determination. *Biometrika, 82*(4), 711–732.

Griffin, J. M., and Schulman, C. T. (2005). Price asymmetry in energy demand models: A proxy for energy-saving technical change? *The Energy Journal, 26*(2), 1–21.

Haldenbilen, S. (2006). Fuel price determination in transportation sector using predicted energy and transport demand. *Energy Policy, 34*(17), 3078–3086.

Hanley, N., McGregor, P. G., Swales, J. K., and Turner, K. (2009). Do increases in energy efficiency improve environmental quality and sustainability? *Ecological Economics, 68*(3), 692–709.

Hansen, M., and Huang, Y. (1997). Road supply and traffic in California urban areas. *Transportation Research Part A: Policy and Practice, 31*(3), 205–218.

Hausman, J. A. (1978). Specification tests in econometrics. *Econometrica: Journal of the Econometric Society, 46*(6), 1251–1271.

Hoeting, J. A., Madigan, D., Raftery, A. E., and Volinsky, C. T. (1999). Bayesian model averaging: A tutorial. *Statistical Science, 14*(4), 382–401.

Hofer, C., Dresner, M. E., and Windle, R. J. (2010). The environmental effects of airline carbon emissions taxation in the US. *Transportation Research Part D: Transport and Environment, 15*(1), 37–45.

Hogan, W. W. (1993). OECD oil demand dynamics: Trends and asymmetries. *The Energy Journal, 14*(1), 125–157.

Hyndman, R. J., Akram, M., and Archibald, B. C. (2008). The admissible parameter space for exponential smoothing models. *Annals of the Institute of Statistical Mathematics, 60*(2), 407–426.

Hyndman, R. J., and Khandakar, Y. (2007). Automatic time series forecasting: The forecast package for R 7. 2008. Available at: https://jstatsoft.org/article/view/v027i03 [accessed 2016–2002–2024][WebCite Cache]

Hyndman, R. J., Koehler, A. B., Snyder, R. D., and Grose, S. (2002). A state space framework for automatic forecasting using exponential smoothing methods. *International Journal of Forecasting, 18*(3), 439–454.

International Energy Agency (IEA) (2015). 2013 Energy Balance for China [DB/OL]. Available at: www.iea.org/statistics/statisticssearch/report/?country=China&product=balances

Janić, M. (2014). Greening commercial air transportation by using liquid hydrogen (LH 2) as a fuel. *International Journal of Hydrogen Energy, 39*(29), 16426–16441.

Kennedy, D., and Wallis, I. (2007). Impacts of fuel price changes on New Zealand transport. *Land Transport New Zealand*. Available at: www.nzta.govt.nz/.

Kick, T., Herbst, J., Kathrotia, T., Marquetand, J., Braun-Unkhoff, M., Naumann, C., and Riedel, U. (2012). An experimental and modeling study of burning velocities of possible future synthetic jet fuels. *Energy*, *43*(1), 111–123.

Kim, J., and Moon, I. (2008). The role of hydrogen in the road transportation sector for a sustainable energy system: A case study of Korea. *International Journal of Hydrogen Energy*, *33*(24), 7326–7337.

Koehler, A. B., Snyder, R. D., Ord, J. K., and Beaumont, A. (2012). A study of outliers in the exponential smoothing approach to forecasting. *International Journal of Forecasting*, *28*(2), 477–484.

Kong, X. (2010). China's coal consumption and the factors influencing the dynamic relationship between the empirical analysis, and theory of coal consumption of asymmetric price effect. *Journal of Resources Science*, *32*(10), 1830–1838 (In Chinese)

Kunert, U., and Kuhfeld, H. (2007). The diverse structures of passenger car taxation in Europe and the EU Commissions proposal for reform. *Transport Policy*, *14*(4), 306–316.

Kurz-Kim, J. R. (2008). Combining forecasts using optimal combination weight and generalized autoregression. *Journal of Forecasting*, *27*(5), 419–432.

Leamer, E. E. (1978). *Specification searches.* New York: Wiley.

Litman, T. (2011). *Evaluating accessibility for transportation planning.* Victoria, BC: Victoria Transport Policy Institute.

Liu, J., Chen, W., and Lin, D. (2011). China ESDPM model and its application in transport demand projection. *China Population Resources and Environment*, *21*(3), 71–75. (In Chinese)

Liu, Y. (2009). Exploring the relationship between urbanization and energy consumption in China using ARDL (autoregressive distributed lag) and FDM (factor decomposition model). *Energy*, *34*(11), 1846–1854.

Mazraati, M. (2009). World aviation fuel demand outlook. *OPEC Energy Review*, *34*(1), 42–72.

Mazraati, M., and Alyousif, O. M. (2009). Aviation fuel demand modelling in OECD and developing countries: impacts of fuel efficiency. *OPEC Energy Review*, *33*(1), 23–46.

Mazraati, M., and Faquih, Y. O. (2008). Modelling aviation fuel demand: The case of the United States and China. *OPEC Energy Review*, *32*(4), 323–342.

Meade, N. (2000). Evidence for the selection of forecasting methods. *Journal of Forecasting*, *19*(6), 515–535.

Ministry of Environmental Protection (n.d.) *Annals of China's Motor Vehicle Pollution Prevention of 2013.* Available at: http://www.mep.gov.cn/gkml/hbb/qt/201401/W020140126591490573172.pdf

Ministry of Transport (2013). *China Transportation Yearbook.* Beijing: Yearbook of China Transportation & Communications.

Musso, A., Piccioni, C., Tozzi, M., Godard, G., Lapeyre, A., and Papandreou, K. (2013). Road transport elasticity: How fuel price changes can affect traffic demand on a toll motorway. *Procedia-Social and Behavioral Sciences*, *87*, 85–102.

Novak, D. C., and McDonald, M. (1998). A general overview of the potential macroeconomic impacts of ITS investment in the United States. Available at: https://trid.trb.org/view.aspx?id=682017

Nygren, E., Aleklett, K., and Höök, M. (2009). Aviation fuel and future oil production scenarios. *Energy Policy*, *37*(10), 4003–4010.

Orturzar, J.D. de, and L.G. Willumsen (2006). *Modelling Transport* (3th edition), Chichester: John Wiley and Sons.

Paulley, N., Balcombe, R., Mackett, R., Titheridge, H., Preston, J., Wardman, M., . . . and White, P. (2006). The demand for public transport: the effects of fares, quality of service, income and car ownership. *Transport Policy*, *13*(4), 295–306.

Penner, J. E. (1999). Aviation Activities and Global Climate. Available at: www.ipcc.ch/ipccreports/sres/aviation/index.php?idp=0

Schafer, A. (1998). The global demand for motorized mobility. *Transportation Research Part A: Policy and Practice*, *32*(6), 455–477.

Sentenac-Chemin, E. (2012). Is the price effect on fuel consumption symmetric? Some evidence from an empirical study. *Energy Policy*, *41*, 59–65.

Shi, L. X. (2011). Recommendations to transport energy saving and emissions reduction in China. In *Study of transport energy consumption and carbon emissions* (pp. 2–3). Beijing: China Economic Publishing House. (In Chinese)

Shunping, J. I. A., Baohua, M. A. O., Shuang, L. I. U., and Qipeng, S. U. N. (2010). Calculation and analysis of transportation energy consumption level in China. *Journal of Transportation Systems Engineering and Information Technology*, *10*(1), 22–27.

Small, K. A., and Van Dender, K. (2007). Long run trends in transport demand, fuel price elasticities and implications of the oil outlook for transport policy. Available at: www.oecd-ilibrary.org/transport/long-run-trends-in-transport-demand-fuel-price-elasticities-and-implications-of-the-oil-outlook-for-transport-policy_234582117245

Sterner, T. (2007). Fuel taxes: an important instrument for climate policy. *Energy Policy*, *35*(6), 3194–3202.

Sun, Q., Jia, S., Zhu, L., and Xu, C. (2013). Dynamic situation combination decomposition model of urban traffic energy consumption. *Journal of Traffic Transportation Engineering*, *13*(3), 94–100. (In Chinese)

Taylor, J. W. (2004). Smooth transition exponential smoothing. *Journal of Forecasting*, *23*(6), 385–404.

Tillema, T., Ben-Elia, E., Ettema, D., and van Delden, J. (2013). Charging versus rewarding: A comparison of road-pricing and rewarding peak avoidance in the Netherlands. *Transport Policy*, *26*, 4–14.

Traill, B., Colman, D., and Young, T. (1978). Estimating irreversible supply functions. *American Journal of Agricultural Economics*, *60*(3), 528–531.

Viallefont, V., Raftery, A. E., and Richardson, S. (2001). Variable selection and Bayesian model averaging in case-control studies. *Statistics in Medicine*, *20*(21), 3215–3230.

Wadud, Z., Graham, D. J., and Noland, R. B. (2009). Modelling fuel demand for different socio-economic groups. *Applied Energy*, *86*(12), 2740–2749.

Walker, I. O., and Wirl, F. (1993). Irreversible price-induced efficiency improvements: Theory and empirical application to road transportation. *The Energy Journal*, *14*(4), 183–205.

Wang, Y. F., Li, K. P., Xu, X. M., and Zhang, Y. R. (2014). Transport energy consumption and saving in China. *Renewable and Sustainable Energy Reviews*, *29*, 641–655.

Wang, Y. F., Zhu, X., Li, L., and Wu, B. (2013). Integrated multimodal metropolitan transportation model. *Procedia-Social and Behavioral Sciences*, *96*, 2138–2146.

Wang, Z., and Lu, M. (2014). An empirical study of direct rebound effect for road freight transport in China. *Applied Energy*, *133*, 274–281.

Wei, Q. Q., Zhao, S. Z., and Xiao, W. (2013). An empirical study of energy prices effect on transportation energy intensity in China. *Ecological Economy*, 2, 018.

Wei, Q. Q., Zhao, S. Z., and Xiao, W. (2014). A quantitative analysis of their impact on energy intensity of transportation structure optimization in China. *Statistics and Decision*, 4, 117–119. (In Chinese)

Wells, A. T. (1988). *Air Transportation: A Management Perspective* (pp. 50–51). Canada: Wadsworth Publishing Company.

WIND Database (n.d.). Available at: http://www.wind.com.cn/NewSite/edb.html

Wolffram, R. (1971). Positivistic measures of aggregate supply elasticities: Some new approaches – some critical notes. *American Journal of Agricultural Economics*, 53(2), 356–359.

World Bank, Carbon Dioxide Information Analysis Center (n.d.). CO2 emissions (metric tons per capita) – China. Available at: http://data.worldbank.org/indicator/EN.ATM.CO2E.PC

World Health Organization (n.d.). *Guidelines for Air Quality*. Available at: http://apps.who.int/iris/bitstream/10665/66537/17/7117055855-chi.pdf?ua=1 (in Chinese)

Wright, S. (1921). Correlation and causation. *Journal of Agricultural Research*, 20(7), 557–585.

Wu, K. Y., He, C. H., Wang, G. X., and Zhang, H. (2012). Measurement and composition analysis on carbon emissions of transportation industry in Shanghai. *Economic Geography*, 11, 45–51. (In Chinese)

Yan, X., and Crookes, R. J. (2010). Energy demand and emissions from road transportation vehicles in China. *Progress in Energy and Combustion Science*, 36(6), 651–676.

Zhang, L., Rong, J., Chen, L., and He, Y. (2006). Feasibility analysis of congestion pricing in Beijing. *Journal of Transportation on Systems Engineering and Information Technology*, 6(2), 124–128. (In Chinese)

Zhang, Q., Tao, X. M., and Yang, P. (2012). Research on carbon emissions from metropolis urban passenger transport and countermeasures. *China Population, Resources and Environment*, 11, 35–42. (In Chinese)

Zhang, Y., Xiong, X. P., Kang, Y. B. (2015). Study on influencing factors and carbon emission reduction pathway for transportation sector of China. *Journal Environmental Protection*, 43(11), 54–57.

Zhao, S. B., and Hu, J. Y. (2002). Development trend of aviation oil market. *China Industrial Economy*, 5, 34–36. (In Chinese)Zhou, W., Zhu, B., Chen, D., Griffy-Brown, C., Ma, Y., and Fei, W. (2012). Energy consumption patterns in the process of China's urbanization. *Population and Environment*, 33(2–3), 202–220.

Zou, G., and Chau, K. W. (2006). Short-and long-run effects between oil consumption and economic growth in China. *Energy Policy*, 34(18), 3644–3655.

Index

Page numbers in italic format indicate figures and tables.

For Product Safety Concerns and Information please contact our EU
representative GPSR@taylorandfrancis.com
Taylor & Francis Verlag GmbH, Kaufingerstraße 24, 80331 München, Germany